American Man

American Man

Speaking the Truth About
THE WAR ON
MASCULINITY

Lawrence Jones

CENTER
STREET
New York • Nashville

Center Street
Hachette Book Group
1290 Avenue of the Americas, New York, NY 10104
centerstreet.com
twitter.com/centerstreet

First Edition: October 2023

Center Street is a division of Hachette Book Group, Inc. The Center Street name and logo are trademarks of Hachette Book Group, Inc.

The publisher is not responsible for websites (or their content) that are not owned by the publisher.

The Hachette Speakers Bureau provides a wide range of authors for speaking events. To find out more, go to hachettespeakersbureau.com or email HachetteSpeakers@hbgusa.com.

Center Street books may be purchased in bulk for business, educational, or promotional use. For information, please contact your local bookseller or the Hachette Book Group Special Markets Department at special.markets@hbgusa.com.

Scripture quotations are taken from the New King James Version of the Bible.

Library of Congress Cataloging-in-Publication Data

Names: Jones, Lawrence, 1992– author.

Title: American man : speaking the truth about the war on masculinity / Lawrence Jones.

Description: First edition. | New York : Center Street, 2023. | Includes bibliographical references.

Identifiers: LCCN 2023020950 | ISBN 9781546005445 (hardcover) | ISBN 9781546005469 (ebook)

Subjects: LCSH: Masculinity—United States. | Men—United States—Identity.

Classification: LCC HQ1090.3 .J663 2023 | DDC 305.310973—dc23/eng/20230607

LC record available at https://lccn.loc.gov/2023020950

ISBNs: 9781546005445 (hardcover), 9781546005469 (ebook)

Printed in the United States of America

LAKE

10 9 8 7 6 5 4 3 2 1

Dedicated to the people that made me into an
American Man... Mama and Daddy

Contents

The War on Masculinity

My Fox News colleague Will Cain, a fellow Texan, had a question for me that I wasn't anticipating. He asked how did I, Lawrence Jones, get where I am? What was it about my background that propelled me to succeed? When Will asked me this on his podcast, I immediately thought of my father. Dad may have been something of an ass-kicker, but he consciously made sure I had all the tools I needed to be successful. "My techniques were harsh," my father once admitted, "but they guaranteed results."

As I explained the sometimes rocky relationship I had with my father, Will wondered out loud whether his kids thought of him much the same way. Will and I may have disagreed around the edges on just how much discipline is appropriate, but what we agreed on was that all young males need a firm paternal hand to help guide their lives. Unfortunately, too many young men aren't getting one.

That conversation with Will prompted me to write this book. For me, it has been a journey of exploration. It seemed clear to me that traditional notions of manhood were under attack, but I wanted to know who was doing the attacking and why. Whatever those forces were, my father would be the first to tell you that we went wrong by compromising with them. My dad, I have come to see, was on the money.

Here is a thought exercise for anyone who doubts we have compromised too much. Binge-watch the first few seasons of the (surprisingly thoughtful) AMC TV series *The Walking Dead*. After each episode, read from the 2018 update of the publication by the American Psychological Association titled "APA Guidelines for Psychological Practice with Boys and Men." Then compare and contrast.

The Walking Dead debuted in 2010 and was still running until 2022. The series should have wrapped up about eight seasons before it actually did. After the first three or four seasons, the show grew silly, woke, and unwatchable. The first seasons, however, offered the most compelling scenario I've seen of what might happen in the United States if all social order collapsed. For the viewer, especially for young men, those first seasons also present a useful moral guide.

The show's tagline pretty well summarizes the plot. "Sheriff Deputy Rick Grimes wakes up from a coma to learn the world is in ruins and must lead a group of survivors to stay alive." A plague has struck the land. To make matters more harrowing, those who die arise again as zombies with no greater purpose than to bite the living and infect them. To say the least, the "walkers" are a major inconvenience.

One natural consequence of the societal collapse is that gender roles revert to what they had been almost everywhere before the age of modern conveniences. The fact that men are, by and large, bigger, stronger, more technically inclined, and more comfortable with weapons now matters a lot. While doing the wash by hand, one woman complains about her new role, and another responds, "The world ended. Didn't you get the memo?"

Critics of the show didn't get the memo either. They complain of its "patriarchal problem," a symptom in their minds of the "toxic masculinity" allegedly abroad in the land.[1] When I Google the phrase "toxic masculinity," I come up with nearly six million hits. Although feminists use the phrase freely— much too freely—the concept of "toxic masculinity" has its origins in the New Age men's movements of the 1980s and 1990s. I suppose the groups this movement spawned meant well, but they tended to be inner-directed to the point of narcissism, and their net effect was to feminize men.

That feminization has been remarkably successful, certainly among educated elites. For instance, when the American Psychological Association issued its updated "Guidelines," the authors did not feel the need to use the phrase "toxic masculinity."[2] For the APA, "traditional masculinity" serves pretty much the same purpose. The APA's "Guidelines" do not so much anticipate the future as reflect the thinking of the present. The authors define "traditional masculinity" to mean "a particular constellation of standards that have held sway over large segments of the population, including: anti-femininity, achievement, eschewal of the appearance of weakness, and adventure, risk, and violence."

Throughout the lengthy document, the authors speak of traditional masculinity as a pathology, a "harmful" one that needs to be treated. Conforming to masculine standards, we are told, "has been shown to limit males' psychological development, constrain their behavior, result in gender role strain and gender role conflict." The consequences are both personal and societal. On the personal level, this "ideology"—their term—"discourages men from being intimate with others and is the primary reason men tend to have fewer close friends than women." It also causes men to "shy away from directly expressing their vulnerable feelings."

On a societal level, "Traditional masculinity ideologies have also been linked to parenting concerns, including work-family conflicts." Worse still, these ideologies have "been connected to sexual assault perpetration…as well as decreased condom use and increased casual 'hook-up' sex." I know the phrase "follow the money" does not explain everything. That said, when the authors complain that teaching boys "to be self-reliant, strong, and to minimize and manage their problems on their own" produces adult men "who are less willing to seek mental health treatment," I get suspicious.

I'm not aware of any public comments from the APA about *The Walking Dead*, but I can imagine how these shrinks might feel about a show that details the value of traditional masculinity and celebrates it. Rick Grimes emerges as the leader of a cluster that includes his young son and pregnant wife. Others look to him as their leader because he is self-reliant, strong, and solution oriented. He has no time for expressing his vulnerable feelings or making close friends. These are luxuries afforded men only after they have suppressed external threats.

Rick sounds much like the husband of "@conmomma," whose random tweet I stumbled across recently. "I am married to a masculine man," she wrote. "He's 6'5, muscles, beard & carries a gun, but that's not what makes him masculine. He protects, defends, provides, & loves his family. I respect & value him. He also values & respects me. That's what strong masculine men do."[3] Tony Evans, the senior pastor of the Oak Cliff Bible Fellowship in Dallas, has another phrase to describe the nature of this kind of man, "Biblical masculinity."[4]

In truth, the creators of *The Walking Dead* understand masculinity better than do the psychologists of the APA. Of the group's strong male characters, Rick is not the biggest, the strongest, or the most technically inclined. Although strong and competent, Rick is elevated to the leadership role by dint of his other masculine virtues—his restraint, his prudence, his courage, his rationality, all in the face of a genuine existential threat. Through his leadership, his group respects its women, protects its young, and retains its Christian ethos. Rick also helps corral the more reckless impulses of some otherwise valuable males. Their help is essential if the group is to protect itself from other clusters of the living that do not share the values of Rick's group.

Women got the show. Despite the gore and the violence, at the show's prime the audience was more than 40 percent female.[5] In a similar vein, I am hoping women will get this book. I do not write about men in a vacuum. They don't exist in a vacuum. I write about men in their relationship to society in general and women in particular. The better women understand the men in their lives—fathers, sons, brothers, friends, husbands, lovers—the better they will be able to navigate the world around them. As an added bonus, this book has far less violence than *The Walking Dead* and absolutely no gore!

Although *The Walking Dead* is not overtly Christian, Rick embodies what Evans calls "the Kingdom man." Says Evans, "He accepts the responsibility to fulfill his God-given role," and that role "is to be a responsible protector and provider with integrity for those whom God placed under his charge."

Not expecting a zombie apocalypse anytime soon, I write this book to counter the feminization of our young men. I believe that boys should be taught from an early age to be strong and self-reliant problem solvers. As Proverbs 22:6 reminds us, "Train up a child in the way he should go, And when he is old, he will not depart from it." That is how my father taught me, and although we don't see eye to eye on everything, self-reliance is one thing we do agree on. My dad never stopped teaching. Always provide for your family, he would tell me. Mediocrity is not an option. Always be there for your children. Knowledge is power. Sleeping in makes your house stink. Always look a man in the eye. I could go on for days.

Without that kind of father-to-son transmission, the virtues associated with traditional masculinity such as courage, strength, perseverance, resilience, and self-reliance will be as missing from society as they are from the APA document. (There is hardly any reference at all to any such virtue in the "Guidelines.") And if men are less open about their feelings and have fewer close friends than women, there is a reason for that, a simple one: Men are different from women. In the immortal words of Homer Simpson, "D'oh!" Women may be different, but they are not less. They are different in a good way. From my mother I learned humility, love, grace, forgiveness, charity— the bedrock virtues of our Judeo-Christian legacy.

The point of this book is not to stroke men's egos. Our egos get stroked enough. And I have certainly no desire to demean women. I come from a generation whose women have smashed one glass ceiling after another. In fact, I think that a man can find no better partner in life than a woman who is strong and competent. If she has a few scars on her hands from shattering glass, I say all the better.

That said, just because a woman can do something does not mean she should. As my actor friend Dean Cain tells me, "There is male energy. There is female energy. Sometimes they commingle, and sometimes they don't, but it's happened for thousands and thousands of years, and there's a reason for this."[6]

Society is pushing women into roles that men can do better and pushing men out to accommodate them. To cite one example, Democrats in the state of Connecticut have proposed a bill that would allow women to bypass the physical ability test for firefighters.[7] This kind of thinking benefits no one—not the women hired, not the men rejected, and certainly not the citizens hoping to be rescued when their homes are on fire.

If society has gotten something this obvious so fundamentally wrong, men must bear a good share of the blame. By failing to live up to our responsibilities as fathers and providers, we have left a cultural void that woke ideologues have been happy to fill. Unfortunately, the proposed solutions have been catastrophic. My fear is that if we continue down this path, utter chaos will follow.

Many of these ideologies were nurtured on America's college campuses. I was first exposed to them when I ran *Campus Reform*, an organization that focuses on common sense and free speech issues. In 2017, for instance, we reported on a flourishing "men's project" at Northwestern University that asked male students to "deconstruct their own masculinity."[8] The Men's Project at the University of Connecticut, all too predictably, is hosted by the Women's Center. One of its programs that we highlighted was designed to help males overcome "mansplaining" and "interrupting others."[9] Meanwhile Missouri State University set up a program to handle that all-purpose pathology, "toxic masculinity."[10]

It will surprise no one that the ideologues ignore what I consider the most toxic of male gestures, passing oneself off as a female in order to dominate women in sports and in other environments—prison, for instance—where males have a natural advantage. Not too long ago society understood such exploitation was simply wrong. If proof were needed, I would recommend the reader watch the 2002 film *Juwanna Mann*. As the plot unfolds, star basketball player Jamal Jeffries is dropped by his team in a fictionalized NBA for his selfish and erratic behavior. Swimming in debt, Jeffries decides to pass himself off as a woman named Juwanna Mann and joins the Charlotte Banshees in the WNBA equivalent. There he dominates. In the championship game, he steals a ball in the closing seconds. Forgetting himself, he flies down the court and ends the game with a backboard-shattering slam dunk, in the course of which his wig falls off.

Everyone sees that he is actually Jamal Jeffries. His teammates are horrified. They feel betrayed. One calls his deceit "straight-up sicko." A sportscaster thinks a man impersonating a woman "the most bizarre sports story ever." Jay Leno mocks Jeffries on late-night TV. Although more sincere, Renée Richards, born Richard Raskind, faced nearly comparable pushback when competing in pro tennis as a forty-two-year-old female in 1977. Those objecting weren't bigots. They just understood the unfairness of it all, the toxicity of exploiting one's maleness to deny women their rightful due.

A generation ago it was understood that each sex was unique, special, and designed by God to be that way. Now, not even a Supreme Court nominee dares to say out loud what a woman is. Justice Ketanji Brown Jackson knew the truth, as do we, but we also know that there is a mob waiting to cancel us or worse if we say the truth out loud.[11]

As a libertarian I struggled with this issue because I value freedom and liberty, but as my Fox News colleague Mark Levin reminds me, "Liberty allows evil people to do evil things."[12] To counter the evil, good people have to step up. But where are the sincere feminists? Where are the fathers who should be protecting their daughters? They are silent not because they agree but because they fear the mob will destroy them. In the immortal words of Dean Cain, "No one has the balls to say it, but the emperor has no clothes on." Our silence isn't love. It's complicity with an agenda that flies in the face of natural law and God's design.

As the reader might expect, there is no reference at all to faith of any kind in the various campus "reforms" or woke mandates, let alone in the "APA Guidelines." "God" has been written out of the ideologues' equations. They propose to remedy some of the very real problems males face without any appeal to God or faith. I don't think we can.

In the pages that follow, I hope to show just how Godliness has helped shape this nation, the most successful in the history of the world. If we are to restore what's best about America and to reach for what we have yet to achieve, I am convinced we will need all the manly virtue we can summon, and we cannot be shy about saying so. The risks we run in speaking out are real, but the risks we run by staying silent are potentially catastrophic.

CHAPTER 1

Man as Father

In 2008, I was working on the Barack Obama campaign when I heard that Tim Russert had died. Although not quite sixteen at the time, I was enough of a political junkie to see how his unexpected death at age fifty-eight shook the political establishment. As the years went on, I came to see how deeply his death affected the American political media. It was never the same again.

Russert, you see, may well have been the last objective journalist on network TV. When guests appeared on the show he hosted, *Meet the Press*, they expected a tough grilling but a fair shake. This took some discipline on his part. He had moved into the political world as a top aide first for

Senator Daniel Patrick Moynihan and later for Governor Mario Cuomo, both Democrats. For the sixteen years Russert hosted *Meet the Press*, the show mattered. It has not mattered since.

Four years before his death, Tim Russert wrote a tribute to his father—also named Tim Russert—titled *Big Russ and Me*. Despite the book's unconventional subject matter, it was a number one *New York Times* bestseller. "I'm forever thankful that my father wrote *Big Russ and Me*," Luke Russert, the broadcaster's son, wrote in the preface of the book's tenth anniversary edition. "Not just because it's a wonderful book, but for the more selfish reason that it has given me my father's playbook as I have embarked on my own life."[1]

In a sentence, Luke sums up why fathers matter. Good fathers write the playbooks for their sons, and good sons refine that playbook and pass it on to their sons. Tim Russert was both good son and good father. His tribute to his father is as clear and as comprehensive a paternal playbook as I have ever seen. As such, it makes a useful launching pad for me to describe my own experience as the son of a man who had many lessons to teach as well.

Unlike in more static cultures, life in America is perpetually in flux. This makes the relationships between fathers and sons more challenging than they have been in other places and at other times. When I was an adolescent, the temperature was often turned up between me and my father. He saw me as a know-it-all. I saw him as, well...I'll hold that thought. As a father, Tim Russert needed some time to come to terms with the fact that "your son is an independent person, rather than a smaller version of you."[2] A son's world is always going to be a little different from that of a father, and a father has to respect that difference.

At the same time, the father has to be the one who calls the shots. Pastor Evans talks about how he chafed under his father's restrictions. Like all sons from time immemorial, he wanted more freedom than his father was willing to grant. His father did not shy away from reminding him that as long as he lived in his parents' house, there were going to be limits to his freedom. "I'm big dog, you're little puppy," his father told him. Tony got the message.[3]

When I ask my Fox News colleague Mark Levin what he learned from his father, he answers, "I learned everything from my father...and my mother." Although Russert grew up Catholic in Buffalo and I Protestant in suburban Dallas and Levin Jewish in Philadelphia, we share the same Judeo-Christian ethos that has defined American culture since the founding. "The most important lesson," Mark tells me, "was to be a moral human being, to have integrity and honor, to respect people, particularly people who are less fortunate than you."

Like Russert, I, too, bear my father's name. He is Lawrence Jones II, I Lawrence Jones III. The lessons his father taught him are very much like the lessons my father taught me. The goal of our fathers in both cases was to mold us into men capable of navigating the world of opportunity every American boy faces. For many a father, it's not just about molding but about making sure his sons can mold their own families when that time comes. It is about preserving the bloodline and the family name. Mark Levin agrees. "If you're a man, if you have children and grandchildren," he tells me, "they are *your* responsibility. That comes down from the ages." He adds, "It is your job to teach your boy to become a man."

For all the commonalities among American men, the lesson each father teaches his sons is unique. When my father was a boy, Texas was just emerging from its segregationist phase. He has enormous respect for those older Black people who endured Jim Crow and helped break down the barriers. He demanded that we respect these people as well and show them deference. If we saw, say, a Black elder struggling to get a jar off a high shelf at a Walmart, he would tell us, "Speak to them. Ask them if there is anything they need. They paid the price."

Big Russ paid his price as well. He was of the generation we call the "greatest," a designation that generation deserves. The young men of that generation were tested first by the Great Depression and then by war. Big Russ was one of them. An Irish-American high school dropout from South Buffalo, he gave up several years of his life to the United States Army Air Forces. Although working on the ground crew out of a base in England, he spent enough time airborne to survive the flaming crash of a B-24 Liberator. He was one of the few who survived that crash.

Like so many men of that generation, Big Russ chose not to talk about his experience until his son forced the story out of him. Upon reading a newspaper clipping about his survival, Tim told Big Russ he thought the story amazing. "It was a lot tougher for the guys who died," said Big Russ and put the clipping away. End of story. "Dad's bravery and his stoicism are in such stark contrast to the scenes we see played out every day in newspapers and on television," writes Russert, "where people can't wait to describe their pain and their agony in front of an audience."[4]

At war's end, Big Russ and other men like him returned home and began their lives over, wiser for the experience. The media encourage us to write off the fifties as a time of complacency in the face of the many injustices still at large in America, but Big Russ had a more realistic take on that period. "They wanted community," he told his son about his fellow veterans. "They wanted a home. They wanted a good reputation with their kids. What's the old saying? 'Your nose to the grindstone and hope for the best.'"[5]

Big Russ took a job with the sanitation department for the security it offered and worked another job on the side, as most workingmen did, to support his growing family. Tim, who was born in 1950, was one of four children, the median size for a family in South Buffalo at that time. Family size would peak in about 1960 and has been declining ever since. The refusal of men to embrace fatherhood is not a healthy sign for the culture.

The lessons that fathers impart to their sons about being a man flow out of everyday experience, which is why just being there is so important. Every family's history is different. Russert tells a story about breaking a neighbor's window while playing baseball. He reported the incident to his mother, who, in turn, referred him to his father. "Look, the first thing you have to do is go over there and tell him you did it," said Big Russ. "You also have to pay for it out of your own money." Russert did as instructed and told the man he would pay to replace the window. When he asked for the ball back, the neighbor refused to return it until the window was fixed.

That afternoon Big Russ bought a pane of glass and installed it, all the while instructing Russert in the proper way to repair a window. "I learned how to dispose of broken glass," Russert writes, "but the real lesson I learned that day was about accountability. If you break somebody's window, it's not enough to fix it. You have to be man enough to go to that person and tell him, to his face, what you have done." Russert adds, "Our neighborhood was filled with men like Dad."[6]

As trivial as this incident might seem, imagine how it might have played out in a home without a father, let alone a neighborhood without fathers. The boy breaks a window. No responsible adult sees him do it. The boys all run away laughing. That is what boys do and will always do without a firm hand to guide them.

Just as Big Russ was there for his son, the son was there for his son. "The greatest gift my father ever gave me was his time," writes Luke Russert. "Here was a man who worked seven days a week, rarely slept more than six hours a night, and yet I can never remember a time when he wasn't there for me or didn't make a Herculean effort to be present."[7]

My dad was a workhorse too. He believed that work was essential. If he wasn't physically working to provide for the family, he was working around the house to make sure the engine was clean. And if he was up working, that meant I was up too. I eventually learned to proactively find something to do to avoid the lament "I'm working, so I'm confused as to why you're on your ass."

Many of the lessons fathers teach are simple but essential. "Shaking hands with adults was very important, at least for boys," writes Russert, "and it was something I practiced with Dad until it became second nature." His father insisted on a firm handshake and worked with his son until he mastered it. Understanding the value of a manly handshake, Russert instructed Luke as his father had instructed him. Another practice Russert learned from Big Russ and passed along to Luke was calling one's elders "Sir" or "Ma'am." "It's all about making a good impression and showing respect to other people," Russert explains.[8]

More important than manners were the values that a father passes along to a son. In the Russert home, one such value was education. The fact that Big Russ never finished high school gave him all the more reason for making sure his son followed through. "Doing well in school was expected," writes Russert, "and was not seen as a special achievement. It was part of a broader understanding that if you worked hard and played by the rules, things would generally work out."[9]

Inspired by his parents, Russert won a scholarship to Buffalo's best Catholic high school and went on to graduate from college and law school. "Self-esteem wasn't something you started out with," Russert adds. "It was a feeling that you earned through hard work."[10] In Russert's time, kids were allowed to lose. They had to learn how to accept defeat and how to win graciously. These traits did not come naturally. Today, even at the professional level, you see athletes crying when they lose. When I see this, I suspect that no one was around to teach them otherwise.

Big Russ also knew the value of a dollar and made sure his son did as well. When Russert asked his father for money, Big Russ routinely insisted that his son do something to deserve it like, say, wash the car. He also instructed Russert in the risks of borrowing and warned him against making a habit of it. "You're going to have to pay those off, you know," he warned his son. Arguing from an altruistic perspective, Big Russ made his son aware that if he failed to repay the loans, there would be less opportunity for those coming up behind him to borrow. So instructed, Russert made paying off his loans a priority.[11]

As happens often in America, the son surpasses the father, at least in terms of income. In Russert's case, he went well beyond his father. To repay Big Russ for his years of privation putting him through school, he offered to buy his father a car, any car. To encourage Big Russ, he sent him catalogs from Lexus, Mercedes, even Cadillac. Big Russ was not about to let his son's success spoil him. He bought a Ford. "He had no interest in stepping out of character or in becoming somebody he wasn't," writes Russert. "Even in receiving a gift, Big Russ was teaching me a lesson."[12]

My dad was forever teaching me as well and on this very same subject. If he ever saw me dressing too fashionably for his taste—he wore things until they fell apart—he would caution me, "Don't be too flashy." He was one of those dads who believed that your identity was not determined by what you wore or what kind of car you drove. His character tests were more fundamental. You should look a man in the eyes when speaking, he taught us, and interact with everyone as equals. He would quiz us on our interactions, and I always felt like he was watching me to see if I was applying his teachings as intended.

Later in life, while working for Fox News, I secured an interview with President Donald Trump. Of course, I called my father to discuss the interview beforehand. The president was notorious for bulldozing interviews not just with his ability to physically intimidate the interviewer but also with his willingness to talk over the interviewer. My daddy had only one piece of advice: "That better not happen to you!"

Before going into the interview—just a little nervous, I'll admit—I was listening to one of my favorite rappers. The Secret Service people were mystified, but my camera crew wasn't. They laughed, knowing it was my way of establishing control of the room. I had one other advantage. Although the former president is tall, I'm taller. The moment he walked into the room, I ignored all the advice well-meaning executives had given and remembered the simple advice from my father: Don't let yourself be bulldozed. I wasn't, and I think Trump respected that.

Young men need fathers. When I read that something like 78 percent of all pro athletes go bankrupt within three years of retirement,[13] I suspect that many of them had no one like my father at home to guide them. What often happens, financial advisor Craig Brown said recently on Fox Business, is that family members lean on the athletes for help. This, I know, would strike my father as an inversion of the natural order of things, especially given the short and precarious nature of an athlete's career.

One other lesson that Big Russ shared with his son is one my father shared with me, namely the value of looking at all sides of an issue. Russert attended college in the late 1960s and early 1970s when the issues were hot and the campuses inflamed, often literally. In May 1970, not far from Russert's college in Cleveland, National Guardsmen shot and killed four students at Kent State University. Russert called home, shouting into the phone, "Dad, they're killing us." Big Russ talked sense to his son. "No!" he shouted. "Don't ever say that. A guardsman may have lost his head, but they're not trying to kill you."[14]

Russert did not want to hear what his father had said, but the words seeped in. The next day, he found himself echoing Big Russ's sentiments during a debate at the Student Union. "Four students lost their lives, and I'm sure the guardsmen who shot them feel awful," Russert dared to say. "They're kids, too, and none of them should be the object of our scorn." Unfortunately, today there is no such moderation in campus debates. In fact, debate is all but taboo on America's campuses. Everyone knows everything.

As an adolescent, I thought I knew everything too. I actively campaigned for Barack Obama, but my dad cautioned me to look more carefully at what Obama stood for. He questioned whether Obama's politics aligned with my own faith, and he counseled me to speak with Pastor Tony Evans, a spiritual force in our life and in the nation's. Although I resisted my father's advice much as Russert resisted his father's, the message made sense. In 2012, the first year I was old enough to vote, I voted for Mitt Romney.

In Big Russ's time, Democrats were allowed to be patriots. Although he had his share of questions about the War in Vietnam, Big Russ had no tolerance for protestors who burned the American flag or rooted for the Communists to win. His son learned well. When Russert returned to college in the fall of 1970, he found himself internalizing the message from his father that he had first resisted, namely, "We can be for peace without supporting the enemy. We can be against this war without rooting for the other side."[15] I wonder if the younger Russert could align himself with Democrats of today who have a hard time even faking patriotism.

Perhaps the most important value a father can impart to a son is the value of faith. In the Russert household, faith was front and center. There were crucifixes above every bed, a statue of the Virgin Mary in the backyard, a picture of Jesus's Sacred Heart on the wall, grace before every meal, and prayers before every bedtime. "Religion was serious business," writes Russert.

His parents sacrificed to send all four children to Catholic schools. They honored all the Catholic rituals as a family and attended Mass every Sunday. In his memoir, Russert writes lovingly and at length about the quiet glories of a Catholic childhood. As an adult, in a political party increasingly hostile to Christianity, Tim Russert did not try to hide his Catholicism. Just the opposite, in fact. In the book, for instance, he speaks movingly of how he arranged to have Pope John Paul II kiss his then baby son, Luke. "Even today," he writes, "when I see that picture of the Pope kissing our little boy, I still get choked up."[16]

His son, Luke, sustained the family faith as well. In fact, he attributes much of his father's success as host of *Meet the Press* to his religious grounding and his servant's heart. "He viewed his job as an opportunity to serve, to instruct and hold those with so much power to the highest standards," writes Luke. "He did not do this for money, personal fame, or professional accolades; he did it because, through faith, he carried the conviction that he must ask the important questions on behalf of the American people."[17]

There is, however, one very important question that Tim Russert never asked himself, certainly not in the book about his father, namely, how could he support a political party that was all in for abortion. The Catholic Church could not be clearer in its condemnation of abortion. Pope John Paul II openly called abortion "murder." In his 1995 encyclical, *Evangelium Vitae*,[18] the pope wrote that abortion "always constitutes a grave moral disorder, since it is the deliberate killing of an innocent human being." Even liberal Pope Francis has not wavered on this position. Says Pastor Tony Evans, "When you attack the unborn, you attack God."[19]

In *Evangelium Vitae*, Pope John Paul II goes into great length describing the obligation of political leaders to speak out against abortion and use their leverage to end the practice. It is almost as though this encyclical were written for former New York Governor Mario Cuomo, who did neither. In a famous speech at the University of Notre Dame in 1984, the practicing Catholic Cuomo used every logical fallacy in the book to justify his willingness to identify with a party that condoned the murder of the unborn.[20]

Cuomo was kidding himself and confusing Catholics. The pope made no bones about the Church's position. "Abortion and euthanasia are thus crimes which no human law can claim to legitimize," he wrote. "There is no obligation in conscience to obey such laws; instead there is a grave and clear obligation to oppose them by conscientious objection."[21] At the time of the Notre Dame speech, Russert was a top aide for Cuomo. He makes no mention of the speech in his memoir.

I am reminded here of how famed abolitionist and former slave Frederick Douglass felt about Christians who cherry-picked the Bible to support slavery. "A slaveholder's profession of Christianity is a palpable imposture," said Douglass. "He is a felon of the highest grade. He is a man-stealer. It is of no importance what you put in the other scale."[22] Douglass had more respect for those slaveholders who did not try to justify their iniquity with Christian doctrine.

Russert's book is as warm and as deeply Christian as any book that has ever come out of Washington. I recommend it highly. I would not do so if I thought that he or even Cuomo bear the moral burden of a slaveholder. I do believe, however, that they and other Christian Democrats are as morally compromised on the abortion issue as were those prominent citizens of the North who opposed slavery but not to the point of rocking the boat.

I do not know how Big Russ felt about abortion. His son never told us, but I do know how my parents felt. They not only talked the talk. They walked the walk. When my mother was sixteen and my father eighteen, they made love—my mother for the first time—and they won the Lotto. I doubt if they considered themselves lucky at that moment, but in retrospect, I certainly do. As I told my mother during a live interview on Fox News, "I am so grateful you made that decision because I wouldn't be here today if it wasn't for my momma."[23]

The "decision" I refer to was my mother's refusal to get an abortion. She was sixteen and my father eighteen. My father provided the initial security that my mother needed to make the decision of life and death. More than that, he "manned up"—a phrase that is never more accurate than in this context—and married my mom. My entire future was shaped by the fact that my father stepped up to the plate. For all the lessons that a father can teach his son, none is more valuable than this—the need to take full responsibility for the life of a child he has helped create.

The fact is many men aren't taking their rightful place here. We have lost an entire generation to abortion and are losing still another. Abortion was once reserved for emergency circumstances. Unfortunately, this act is now celebrated. The overturning of *Roe v. Wade* has turned pro-choice advocates into pro-abortion activists. At the 2023 State of the Union Address, for instance, several members of Congress showed up wearing "Abortion" pins—with the "A" in the shape of the heart—where they once might have worn American flag pins.

But if we are to be honest, we men bear our own share of the blame. By abdicating our responsibilities, we threw the door open to those who will not be satisfied until federal abortion laws allow infanticide. Some states already have such laws. If more men would rise to the moment, we wouldn't be where we are today.

No one understood this better than former President Barack Obama. He had been abandoned by his own father at a very early age and often shared that experience with others, most notably on Father's Day of 2008 when he made the best speech of his career. With the Democratic primary campaign behind him, Obama was now directing his message to the general population. More immediately, he was speaking to the congregation at the Apostolic Church of God in Chicago. If anyone appreciated the wisdom of his words, it was these very people. Few in America suffered the consequences of widespread fatherlessness more directly than Chicago's Black American population.

"Here at Apostolic, you are blessed to worship in a house that has been founded on the rock of Jesus Christ, our Lord and Savior," said the future president, affirming the role that faith has played in the Black community.[24] "Of all the rocks upon which we build our lives," Obama continued, "we are reminded today that family is the most important. And we are called to recognize and honor how critical every father is to that foundation." To this point, the ideologues in the audience would not have been troubled. This kind of benign boilerplate had become routine in both parties. But Obama pressed on.

I can imagine the political people beginning to squirm when Obama scolded the missing fathers for having "abandoned their responsibilities, acting like boys instead of men." Then Obama moved into forbidden territory. He acknowledged that for all the heartbreak that happens in a home when a father leaves, any home, that heartbreak turns into catastrophe in a community where fathers routinely leave. And no community was more vulnerable to this plague than the Black community:

We know that more than half of all black children live in single-parent households, a number that has doubled—doubled—since we were children. We know the statistics—that children who grow up without

15

a father are five times more likely to live in poverty and commit crime; nine times more likely to drop out of schools and twenty times more likely to end up in prison. They are more likely to have behavioral problems, or run away from home or become teenage parents themselves. And the foundations of our community are weaker because of it.

As expected, the media glossed over this speech. For one, they did not want to call attention to the fact that a presidential candidate was campaigning in a church, a conflict with their own preaching on the need for separation between church and state. For another, they knew it would rankle the noisier members of their increasingly left-leaning audiences. But Jesse Jackson noticed. A few weeks later, a hot mic on a Fox News studio picked him up making a threat on Obama's very manhood so brutal I will not repeat it here.

Jackson made a half-hearted apology, but the apology gave him the opportunity to lecture the upstart Obama on the way things worked in Washington. A call for males to take responsibility, a call for males to become men, threatened the whole dependence industry that subsidized Jackson and people like him. Backed by the media, Jackson had his way. Obama never again spoke in any meaningful way about the fatherhood crisis. This was a shame. As a good father himself, no one was better positioned to talk about it.

My Texas friend Jack Brewer understood the culture at street level. Coming of age in the 1990s, he was immersed in music that celebrated random fatherhood. "The whole thing was baby mamas," Brewer explains. "I thought that was cool." A gifted athlete, Brewer played several seasons in the NFL and saw the impact of this trend on guys less grounded than he was. "If you have a culture that is going to embrace baby mamas," he tells me, "why would a woman want to submit to a man," especially since "God is not in man right now."[25]

In the years since, the affliction of fatherlessness has continued to spread beyond our community and into every corner of American society. By the time of the 2020 Census, one out of every four White children was living in a home without two married parents. For Hispanics, the figure was four out of ten. For Black Americans, it was almost two out of every three.[26]

Feminization would be problem enough in a well-ordered society, but the surge of unmoored, fatherless boys flooding into our institutions is causing serious disorder. These boys need men who would stand up for them but who would also stand up *to* them. In school, however, they find such men only in the rarest of cases. What they do find is an educational establishment run largely by women and tilted to the needs of girls.

In a recent *New York Times* op-ed, Thomas Edsall reviews a rash of academic articles confirming what is obvious to anyone paying attention: Boys, especially boys from fatherless homes, are falling behind. They are more likely to act out in school, to be suspended, to be assigned to special ed, to drop out. Males are less likely to graduate from high school or go to college. In fact, females make up nearly 60 percent of all college students. One study that Edsall cites comes to what seems like an obvious conclusion: "Male children born into low-income, single-parent-headed households—which in the vast majority of cases are female-headed households—appear to fare particularly poorly on numerous social and educational outcomes."[27]

Once on their own, the behavior of these young males can be toxic. In their relationships with women, too many are content to remain boys, as in "the boyfriend." Not all boyfriends behave badly, but many do. By most accounts, a nonrelated male in the home is at least ten times more likely to abuse the children in his charge than is a biological father. The boyfriend is much more likely to abuse the female as well.[28]

The irony, of course, is that the same media figures that denounce toxic masculinity are the ones who, by celebrating single-parent households, are responsible for creating a new generation of toxic males. We honor the strength of the women who have put their households on their backs, but in so doing, we've missed the fact that these women break their backs by doing so. Women weren't designed to bear so much burden. They do what they must to survive, but they are left wounded and their sons often go wrong.

Hollywood's ignorance showed itself in 1992 when the hard-charging journalist Murphy Brown, the forty-something feminist lead in the television series of the same name, decided to have a baby. Unmarried, Brown chose to raise the child on her own after the biological father, underground radical Jake Lowenstein, begged off. In that 1992 was an election year, incumbent Vice President Dan Quayle chose to address the issue of Brown's single motherhood.

"Bearing babies irresponsibly is, simply, wrong. Failing to support children one has fathered is wrong," said Quayle in a May 1992 speech. "We must be unequivocal about this. It doesn't help matters when prime-time TV has Murphy Brown—a character who supposedly epitomizes today's intelligent, highly paid professional woman—mocking the importance of fathers by bearing a child alone and calling it just another 'life-style choice.'"[29]

The entertainment world rallied noisily to the support of the creators of the show and actress Candice Bergen, who played Murphy Brown. Although raising a legitimate issue, Quayle met with almost universal derision. On a subsequent episode of *Murphy Brown*, its creators allowed the fictional Brown to rebuke the real-life Dan Quayle. "Unfortunately, it seems that for him, the only acceptable definition of a family is a mother, a father and children," said the sanctimonious Brown to her imagined TV audience. "And in a country where millions of children grow up in nontraditional families, that definition seems painfully unfair."[30]

Of course, the show's creators purposefully misrepresented what Quayle had said and got away with it. No one dared push back. When the Bush-Quayle ticket lost the presidency in a three-way race in 1992, Quayle lost his voice. Hollywood, however, kept on preaching. Having won this battle in the culture wars, the entertainment industry responded with show after show featuring independent career women for whom men were an accessory. As *Time* Magazine noted, "Single mothers soon made their way on TV without issue."[31]

At this point, I would like to clarify the objective of this book. We are not addressing the Murphy Browns of the world, at least not directly. Our target audience is the Jake

Lowensteins. In the show, we learn that Murphy and Jake met when both were arrested during a 1968 protest. They subsequently married, but the marriage lasted only seven days before they split. The two reunited briefly some twenty years later when Jake surfaced from the underground, a reunion that resulted in Murphy's pregnancy. Having decided that fatherhood would interfere with his lifestyle, Jake split again.

The Lowenstein character confirms the wisdom of Camille Paglia, a nail-tough author, professor, and contrarian. "A woman simply is," said Paglia, "but a man must become."[32] The fictional Jake failed the "man" test. Half of us are born male, but a much smaller proportion of that half become men. The ones who do will not do so by accident. They will spend their lives in the constant pursuit of true manhood. True manhood does not include abandoning a child. "If you are man enough to get a woman pregnant," Pastor Evans reminds us, "you should be man enough to take care of the child."[33]

The results of that abandonment can be catastrophic. A 1993 article in the liberal journal *The Atlantic*, provocatively titled "Dan Quayle Was Right," came as a shock to those who dared to read it. As author Barbara Dafoe Whitehead pointed out, "Divorce and out-of-wedlock childbirth are transforming the lives of American children," and not in a good way. In the days when TV shows such as *Father Knows Best* were popular, more than 80 percent of children grew up in a family with two married, biological parents. By the Murphy Brown era, that figure had dropped to 50 percent and was trending down.[34]

Dr. Lauren Miller, a neuropsychologist whom I met on assignment, adds another variable to the equation. "When the family loses the father, the husband, the provider, they lose two parents," Miller tells me. The father's departure, she explains, "forces the mom to carry more weight as a provider to compensate for the loss of the father. Then you have the child losing both parents."[35]

As President Obama noted, the children raised in broken homes do worse on every conceivable metric. They are much more likely to remain poor, to suffer emotional problems, to drop out of school, to get pregnant as teenagers, to commit crime, and to spend time in prison. "Despite this growing body of evidence," Whitehead argued, "it is nearly impossible to discuss changes in family structure without provoking angry protest." The defenders of the status quo almost inevitably accuse even sympathetic analysts of attacking single mothers. They are wrong, and I'm sure the overwhelmed mother who shields her children from the tears she secretly cries at night knows the status quo cannot hold.

In 2002, on the tenth anniversary of the critical *Murphy Brown* episodes, Candice Bergen shocked her peers by defending Quayle. "I never have really said much about the whole episode, which was endless," Bergen told a gathering of television critics. "But his speech was a perfectly intelligent speech about fathers not being dispensable and nobody agreed with that more than I did." This took some courage on Bergen's part, given the oppressive nature of Hollywood groupthink. "I think that all of us feel that family values have to sort of come back front and center," she added.[36]

Despite her good intentions, Bergen's response was classic too little, too late. The media largely ignored her. By this time, the "all families are special" mantra had become accepted wisdom in America's newsrooms. It had also become progressive orthodoxy, most notably within the Democratic Party. In 2008, the surprisingly naive presidential candidate Barack Obama learned this the hard way. In fact, so taboo is it to challenge the fatherless home that none of the websites I reviewed dealing with child abuse highlight the dangers inherent with live-in boyfriends, and few even raise the issue.

Among those who have spoken out are the men's rights activists, MRAs for sort, who have lost custody of their children. In 2013, feminist filmmaker Cassie Jaye, astonished to learn that there existed something as seemingly absurd as a men's rights movement, decided to make a documentary to expose its "dark underbelly." Like other feminists, she had been led to believe that "men have all their rights; they have all the power and privilege."[37] After interviewing any number of MRAs across the country, she had to rethink her biases.

As Jaye discovered, men are relatively reluctant to express their feelings or air their gripes. On this point, the American Psychological Association was right. A cultural emphasis on self-reliance makes it seem unmanly for males to organize around their maleness. The one issue that has driven men to organize is child custody. Courts reflexively favor the child's mother.

The case of Texas dad Jeff Younger would be typical save for the fact that his ex-wife, pediatrician Anne Georgulas, is determined to turn their son James, a twin, into a girl. According to Younger, Georgulas began "transitioning" James when he was two years old. At every step, courts have denied Younger any say in the process. Recently, Georgulas took her sons and moved to California, a "sanctuary" state for transgender children and their families. Younger is convinced that the boy's mother intends to have him chemically castrated. "My blood ran cold when I realized what she had planned for that boy," said Younger, but there was almost nothing he could do about it.[38]

Some of the divorced men Jaye interviewed expressed comparable grief and frustration. So moved was Jaye by her experience with these men that her intended exposé of the men's rights movement turned into a defense of that movement. The movie she produced, *The Red Pill: A Feminist's Journey into the Men's Rights Movement*, alienated much of the feminist community. In a subsequent TED Talk, Jaye deconstructed the notion that men have all the power and the privilege:

> Paternity fraud uniquely affects men. The United States Selective Service in the case of a draft still uniquely affects men. Workplace deaths: disproportionately men. War deaths: overwhelmingly men. Suicide: overwhelmingly men. Sentencing disparity, life expectancy, child custody, child support, false rape allegations, criminal court bias, misandry, failure-to-launch boys falling behind in education, homelessness, veterans issues, infant male genital mutilation, lack of parental choice once a child is conceived, lack of resources for male victims of domestic violence, so many issues that are heartbreaking. These are men's issues, and most people can't name one.

For those who may not know, the phrase "red pill" comes from the 1999 movie *The Matrix*. The character Morpheus describes the "matrix" as "the world that has been pulled over your eyes, to blind you from the truth." The "truth," Morpheus tells acolyte Neo, is that he, like everyone else, was "born into a prison that you can not smell or taste or touch." Morpheus offers Neo the choice of two pills to deal with this reality. The blue pill allows the one who chooses it to "believe whatever you want to believe." If Neo takes the red pill, Morpheus promises to show Neo "how deep the rabbit hole goes." As Neo reaches for the red pill, Morpheus reminds him, "All I am offering is the truth, nothing more."[39]

The truth is that the culture has been waging war on fathers and sons for a half century, maybe more. Too many young males have lost their way, and not just the males from fatherless homes. The almost universal fear of celebrating masculinity has left even males from stable families without useful guidelines or reliable role models.

I am dismayed to see young men so comfortable with taking the back seat and not shouldering their responsibility. When we take our place in society, things change. This past year, I went back to my hometown in Garland, Texas, for a back-to-school drive. The boys, now men, whom I grew up with put the event together. Many of these men came from single-parent households. We all understood that in a world where many of the children participating did not have fathers in the home, we had a responsibility to stand in the gap.

As Frederick Douglass observed nearly two centuries ago, "It is easier to build strong children than to repair broken men."[40] That observation is as true now as it was then. A good father has more value in a son's life than a dozen coaches or teachers. Coaches and teachers repair. A father builds. He is there from day one to guide, to instruct, to serve as a role model. It is a father who teaches a son to respect women, to stand up to bullies, to fight for justice, to tell the truth, to keep his word, and to stay strong in the face of adversity. I was blessed to have a father who was always there even when I didn't want him to be. He refused to abandon his responsibility just because I was a know-it-all.

Turning thirty as I have done while writing this book, I consider myself a work in progress. I have not yet married, nor fathered a child. Nor have I fought in a war, and I pray that I never have to. War surely tests one's manhood, but there are other tests, sometimes just as tough, that all of us will face. For fathers, those tests come more often than any father would like.

My Fox News colleague Pete Hegseth has been to war. He has been awarded two Bronze Stars for his service in Iraq and Afghanistan. And although a platoon leader in Iraq, he tells me, "It is much more important and far more difficult to lead a household."[41]

To refine what Camille Paglia said, it is more helpful to show what a man does than to define what a man is. Any male can be a "guy," but to get beyond the "guy" stage takes a concerted effort. "You can't expect anyone else to take up that responsibility," says Hegseth. That effort takes many forms. All males will face challenges on the path to manhood. Those challenges are as varied as the males that face them.

Universal, though, are the virtues a "man" needs to overcome those challenges. These virtues are as old as mankind itself, and none of them is "toxic."

I write none of this to disparage women. As Pastor Evans has reminded me, "Any abuse or degradation of women is an insult to manhood."[42] With few exceptions, men are not whole without women. Jesus Christ knew this to be true. When challenged by the Pharisees on the subject of divorce, then allowed under Mosaic law, Jesus set the record straight, quoting Genesis 2:24. "Have you not read that He who made *them* at the beginning 'made them male and female,' and said, 'For this reason a man shall leave his father and mother and be joined to his wife, and the two shall become one flesh'?" To clarify this point for the skeptical Pharisees, he added, "So then, they are no longer two but one flesh. Therefore, what God has joined together, let not man separate."[43]

For the two to become one, the male must become a man and embrace the duties of manhood. Women do not want to marry a "guy," let alone a boy. They want to marry a man, someone who will support and protect his wife and children. For some males, manhood is instinctive. Others have to work much harder at it. Even a strong man can stumble. The strongest pick themselves back up. To understand how a male achieves manhood, I have reviewed the literature and studied the lives of a score of individuals worthy of the designation "man." Some of these men I have interviewed. Some I have viewed from afar. One brought me into this world and raised me to be who I am.

I don't have all the answers, but I am willing to ask all the questions. Traveling the country as I have done for Fox

News, I have taken the red pill. In taking it, I have seen how confused people are about masculinity in America and how powerful is the need to set the record straight. "We have to swim upstream," Pastor Evans reminds us. "Whoever owns the family owns society."[44]

CHAPTER 2

Man as Protector

Jacob Albarado, an off-duty Border Patrol agent, was getting a haircut when he received an urgent text from his wife, Trisha, a fourth-grade teacher at Robb Elementary School in Uvalde, Texas. "There's an active shooter," Trisha wrote in the first text, immediately followed by "Help." Albarado borrowed his barber's shotgun and raced to the scene. The institutional response was cautious to the point of negligent, but Albarado had a wife and child at that school, and he was not to be deterred. While the tactical team readied itself, Albarado rushed in and started clearing the hysterical kids from their classroom.[1]

Agent Albarado not only rescued his child, but he also organized a plan with other off-duty law enforcement personnel to rescue other kids in the building. He broke protocol because that day he wasn't just an experienced agent. He was a father. While those in leadership fumbled the ball, Albarado was ready to lay down his life for his child. Contrast this with the actions of those in charge. They waited outside while nineteen kids and two teachers were brutally murdered. They had more than a legal obligation to storm the classroom. They had a moral duty as men. As reporter on the scene, I initially gave them the benefit of the doubt. I was wrong.

Although the instinct to protect one's child is universal, I like to think that, in Texas, the instinct is reinforced by the culture. Ed Chelby spent many a sleepless night after the Uvalde massacre. His daughter attends Saegert Elementary. His wife is a nurse at the same school. As a father, he could *not* do nothing. His role, as he saw it, was to protect his wife and daughter as best he could. So Chelby, an eleven-year U.S. Army vet, volunteered to just stand in front of the school. "I said I would just be out there unarmed to let people know that I'm watching," said Chelby. "Let the parents have a little bit of relief."[2] Although a seemingly simple gesture, the school's parents appreciated it greatly.

When men fail in their duty to protect those in their charge, it falls on women to assume that responsibility. Uvalde provides an example of that too. Law enforcement officers, paralyzed by protocol, restrained and handcuffed a mother whose sons were still in the line of fire. "I told one of the officers, 'I don't need you to protect me. Get away from me. I don't need your protection. If anything, I need you to go in with me to go protect my kids,'" farmworker Angeli Gomez told CBS News. Gomez persuaded a local cop to take the cuffs off. When he did, she rushed into the building to rescue her two young sons. The officers who did nothing were deservedly humiliated.[3]

On an individual level, men everywhere are trained to respond. Most do when their family is at risk. Through the wonder of viral videos, we get to see how this protective instinct plays out in real life, especially in Texas. At a Houston rodeo, a bull threw the eighteen-year-old who was riding it and knocked him unconscious. When the boy's father saw his boy lying lifelessly, he jumped out of the stands and covered his son just as the bull approached to do further damage. The comments on YouTube show just how much people appreciate paternal gestures like this[4]:

This really touched me, as we are a protector of our children, I love this, such a beautiful moment of love. Thank you to the Dad.

My dad ran in front of a moving car just in time to pull my sister out of the road. Neither were hit, but this reminded me of that. Fathers just act when their kids are in danger. Well done to this father.

I ain't never seen a bull fighter as willing to completely sacrifice his body for me as my dad was. Now I'm a father and I know why. God bless dads.

John 15:13 Greater love has no one than this, than to
lay down one's life for his friends.

Not all males would do what these Texas fathers did, but
all men would. A man knows to protect his wife and children. This knowledge is part instinct, part education. People
respond positively when they see this virtue in action, which
accounts for the fan popularity of the film *John Q*. Based *very*
roughly on a real-life incident, the 2002 film tells the story of
John Quincy Archibald (Denzel Washington), a father and
husband who takes a hospital staff hostage to assure that his
son gets a needed heart transplant. The critics were cool to the
film, but the audiences appreciated the father's self-sacrifice
to save his son, despite the lawlessness of his actions.

The fans at the 1992 Olympics in Barcelona responded
with even more passion when they saw the interaction
between Jim Redmond and his son Derek. After tearing his
hamstring, Derek struggled painfully to his feet hell-bent on
finishing the 400-meters semifinal in which he was running.
Powered by his paternal instinct, Jim ran out on the track
and helped the limping Derek across the finish line. Like the
Redmonds themselves, the fans knew the officials would rule
that Derek "did not finish," but the official record here was
not what mattered.

It helps enormously if there is a father around to reinforce
this protective reflex in a son. My father certainly did, and it
starts with seemingly little things. If I was walking with my
mom and my sisters, I was instructed to walk on the street side
to protect the ladies from an errant vehicle or even the splash
from a passing car. At night, Dad told my brother and me that

it was our responsibility to make sure the doors of the house and the garage were locked. If we failed in that duty, there was hell to pay. At a restaurant, with females in attendance, we were never to sit with our backs to the door. We were the protectors.

Dad also schooled us on the need to protect ourselves and our future families from financial insecurity. His guru in this school was Dave Ramsey, the commonsense financial advisor for his millions of radio fans. Ramsey's principles were simple: Save a thousand dollars in cash for your starter emergency fund; pay off all debt except the house; save three to six months of expenses in a fully funded emergency fund; and on and on. Whenever I listened, Ramsey always made sense. So did my father.[5]

Not all boys were as fortunate as my brother and me. Boys with absent or indifferent fathers develop little sense of their roles as protectors. As a result, you see an increasing tendency among criminals to kill women and children as wantonly as they do men. On a less lethal level, I watch with awe these viral videos of young women engaged in vicious brawls while the men laugh and shoot video and do nothing to intervene. Say what you will about the Mafia, but in the past at least they were expected to respect the wives and daughters of their enemies.

I spend most of my time reporting from different cities in America, and one thing is clear. The men that once might have protected their communities are now terrorizing those very communities. The LA-based street gangs, the Crips and the Bloods, once had a rule that women and children were off-limits, but now there's no discretion. Said actor Denzel

Washington on the subject, "If the father is not in the home, the boy will find a father in the streets. I saw it in my generation and every generation before me, and every one ever since. If the streets raise you, then the judge becomes your mother and prison becomes your home."[6]

I know I am sounding old before my time, but too many young males seem proud of their passivity and spinelessness. I have had mixed feelings about the war in Ukraine, but when I saw their young men rush to join the fight, I wondered if our young men would do the same. Polls suggest that more than two-thirds of young males in Britain, France, and Germany would be unwilling to defend their country if attacked. I would expect more from our males, but if Uvalde is any example, our institutions seem to be preparing our young men for submission.

This is not the natural order of things. Fathers have been reinforcing their sons' protective instincts since the beginning of time. The quest to protect wife and child, in fact, has been at the center of world literature at least since Homer composed his epic poem the *Odyssey*, some twenty-seven hundred years ago.

The plot of the *Odyssey* revolves around the epic journey of Odysseus—or Ulysses, as the Romans called him—as he makes his way home from the Trojan Wars. Once secretly back at his native Ithaca, he learns that his wife, Penelope, has been subjected to enormous pressure from rivals who have been plundering his home in his absence. "They keep hanging about our house day after day sacrificing our oxen, sheep, and fat goats for their banquets, and never giving so much as a thought to the quantity of wine they drink," laments

Penelope. "No estate can stand such recklessness, for we have now no Ulysses to protect us. If he were to come again, he and his son would soon have their revenge."[7]

Upon affirming the loyalty of Penelope and his son Telemachus, Ulysses makes short work of the plunderers. That is what men have always done, perhaps not as boldly or bloodily as Ulysses did, but each in his own way. Not all men get a chance to slay a roomful of lusty rivals, but all men have the opportunity to do the little things that show both love and concern. Relationship expert Rachael Pace, who writes for marriage.com, lists twenty signs of such male protectiveness.[8] Some of the signs are simple but suggestive, such as walking on the outside of the sidewalk or walking the female to a door or to a car.

Other signs go deeper. "He is always ready to defend you," writes Pace. If the woman is in physical danger, a man drops everything and runs all risks, regardless of the danger to himself. His defense of the woman in his life, however, goes beyond the physical to the emotional. "He steps up for you if you are verbally abused or threatened in any situation," argues Pace. "He likes you and won't tolerate anybody hurting you."

The woman is always more than the mere passive recipient of the man's assistance. As shrewd as her husband, Penelope demanded proof that her protector was not an impostor. "When she heard the sure proofs Ulysses now gave her," Homer tells us, "she fairly broke down. She flew weeping to his side, flung her arms about his neck, and kissed him." The story continues, "Then Ulysses in his turn melted, and wept as he clasped his dear and faithful wife to his bosom."

Not much has changed in the last twenty-seven hundred years. The oneness of male and female is and always has been a central element of much of the world's best literature. Without that completion, the hero's role is never quite fulfilled. Joseph Campbell has famously described the heroic journey of Ulysses and adventurers like him as the "monomyth"—a young male leaves home, tests himself against a world of challenges, and returns home as a man fully able to protect his family.

Although the theme of returning home and protecting your family is universal, the American experience turned the ordinary citizen into a Ulysses. In much of the rest of the world, Europe included, most inhabitants rarely strayed from where they had grown up. The opening of the New World allowed the bolder inhabitants of the Old World to venture beyond historic limits. After a journey almost as epic as Ulysses's, men arrived, often with their family, in a new land among a native population that wasn't always happy to see them. I refer here not only to people immigrating to America from abroad, but also to Americans migrating to the North from an inhospitable South or migrating to the West from an increasingly crowded East.

Upon arriving in his new land, the individual male was expected to create and sustain a home of his own, usually with minimal assistance from the state, if any. These migrations produced a hardy, self-sustaining population of men. Those who couldn't cut it often turned around and went back to where they came from. Those who stayed gave birth to a new generation that did not doubt they belonged. "The great advantage of the Americans is that they have arrived at a state of democracy without having to endure a democratic revolution," writes Alexis de Tocqueville in his classic *Democracy in America*, "and that they are born equal, instead of becoming so."[9]

For the two-and-a-half centuries of its existence, America has been the most consciously and freely religious country in the Western World. Faith, as de Tocqueville observed, helped temper the excesses that flow from an unrestrained individualism. "They therefore profess their religion without shame and without weakness," he writes of Americans, "but there generally is, even in their zeal, something so indescribably tranquil, methodical, and deliberate, that it would seem as if the head, far more than the heart, brought them to the foot of the altar."[10]

The history books are filled with stories of American males who threw off the internal restraints of their faith and yielded to their passions. These are the chapters we wish weren't there. Many of the chapters today feature young men who did not have a father to school them in the art of manly responsibility. As one young man commented on seeing the bull-riding video mentioned previously, "He is very lucky to have a self sacrificing father, makes me wish mine never walked away from our family." Too many fathers do walk away.

The history books tend to overlook the stories from everyday life, those of the countless millions of American men who did not walk away. These men exercised their freedom, took advantage of their opportunities, and honored their faith. They worked hard to support and protect their families, often under considerable duress.

Appropriately perhaps, baseball, the most American of all games, re-creates the heroic monomyth a thousand times every summer day. It is the *Odyssey* to football's *Iliad*. The player starts at home, tests himself against the pitcher and his eight comrades-in-arms, and if successful, returns home a hero. Historically, it has been a game of fathers and sons. The scene in *Field of Dreams* in which the Kevin Costner character says to his phantom father, "Hey, Dad, wanna have a catch," has left more than a few grown men in tears.

Football, like the *Iliad*, squares up two forces in battle, but like all sports it provides its teaching moments as well. In fact, few movies capture the struggle to live out the monomyth and return home a man as well as *American Underdog*, a 2021 biopic about the life of NFL Hall of Famer Kurt Warner. The starting quarterback for only one season at the unheralded University of Northern Iowa, Warner goes undrafted in the 1994 NFL draft. He tries out for the Green Bay Packers but is cut before the season begins. To support himself, he takes a job stocking shelves at a Cedar Falls Hy-Vee grocery store. On the side, he plays in the Arena Football League with a team called, appropriately enough, the Iowa Barnstormers.

I say "appropriately" here because the movie is less about football than it is about Warner's journey to manhood. The woman with whom he lives, Brenda, is the single mother of two children, one of them blind. Early in their relationship, at least in the film version, Brenda's father takes Kurt aside and asks if he is prepared to take care of Brenda and her children. Kurt says yes, but he loses his way while wandering from one arena to another with the Barnstormers. It is only when he accepts his role as provider and protector for the family that he completes his journey.

In a very real sense, the movie climaxes with Kurt's marriage proposal. In the same year that Kurt marries Brenda, 1997, he recommits to Christianity. Only in marriage, the viewer understands, will Kurt fulfill his role as a Christian father and protector. The film, in fact, shows him in his paternal role weaning his blind stepson away from Brenda's overprotective care.

The movie ends with Warner's debut as a twenty-eight-year-old backup quarterback with the St. Louis Rams. The Super Bowl victories, MVP titles, and Hall of Fame induction ceremony are left for the credit sequence. After his second Super Bowl win nine years after his debut, Warner says in real life, "Everybody's going to be tired of hearing this, but I never get tired of saying it. There's one reason that I'm standing up on this stage today. That's because of my Lord up above. I've got to say thanks to Jesus; you knew I was going to do it, but I've got to do it."[11] In the twenty-five years of their marriage, the Warners have added five additional children.

By any standard, especially Hollywood's, *American Underdog* makes a powerful case for responsible fatherhood. In the real Hollywood, responsible fatherhood is in short supply, which makes the real-life journey of Harold Beckenholdt all the more impressive.

Raised on farms along the Kansas-Oklahoma border, Beckenholdt learned early in his life that the one thing he did not want to be was a farmer. Although his family weathered the Great Depression much better than did the Joads, the fictional Okies of *Grapes of Wrath* fame, Beckenholdt, like the Joads, headed to California to seek fame and fortune.

What Harold wanted to be was an actor. During a brief stop in New York, Harold met Henry Fonda, the star of the film version of *The Grapes of Wrath*. With Fonda as his mentor and his service in the United States Air Force behind him, Harold, wife Jean, and their four-year-old son Ronny headed west. Somewhere along the way, he changed his name to the more marquee-friendly Rance Howard. The year was 1958. The vehicle was a 1952 Plymouth. And Rance's destiny, although he could not have imagined it at the time, was to become hands down the best showbiz dad in Hollywood history.

His sons, Ron and Clint, tell their father's story in the recent mega bestseller *The Boys*. It reads like a primer for what a good father should be and not just in Hollywood. The movies themselves have not historically provided much in the way of guidance to a would-be father. As Rance's granddaughter Bryce Howard observes in the book's Foreword, "I've always been confused by how fathers are portrayed in popular culture as out-of-touch bumbling idiots."[12] Neither father Ron nor grandfather Rance fits that mold. According to Bryce, Rance was a different species altogether. Unusual for a Hollywood dad, he served his sons "not just as their guardian-manager but as their ever-present moral and ethical compass."

This is a critical understanding of a father's role as protector. "Protection" means more than just shielding loved ones from physical harm. "A protector is one who wants to keep his family safe," says Pastor Evans. "He wants to be the filter that makes sure nothing comes into his life or the life of the loved ones that will bring physical or emotional harm."[13]

Filtering out temptation is a hard-enough task for a father in everyday life, but in the movie industry, Rance's thoughtful parenting stands out. Writes Clint, the younger and lesser-known brother, "Mom and Dad zealously protected us from the dark and predatory aspects of the business."[14] As Clint observes, many child actors had no such luck. Their parents were often the predators themselves, pushing the kids beyond their limits and squandering their earnings.

The stories of child actors being exploited by their parents are legion. *Home Alone* star Macaulay Culkin speaks of his stage manager father, Kit, as being abusive and controlling and accuses him of "wanting to break my spirit."[15] Culkin's producers were none too happy with Kit either. "I can take so much harassment, so much extortion, so much blackmail," said one producer. "Enough!"[16] Michael Lohan, the father of *Mean Girls* star Lindsay Lohan, is famously exploitative. "My father is known for talking to the press and selling stories. He loves the attention. In the past he's said I've done drugs, he put my number on the internet," Lohan told the *Daily Mail*. "Who does that? Some of the stuff he's done proves to me he doesn't care about me."[17] Country music prodigy LeAnn Rimes went to court as a seventeen-year-old to recover some of the alleged $8 million in earnings her father, Wilbur, and co-manager, Lyle Walker, had siphoned off.[18]

By contrast, the Howards, according to Clint, "were scrupulously honest about money." Adapting to his role as manager-father took considerable humility on Rance's part. He had come west for the sake of his own career, but it was Ron's career that took off. His son was much in demand as a child actor even before he landed the role that defined him as "Opie," the sheriff's son in *The Andy Griffith Show*. The enormously popular show first aired long before my time on this planet, but even to this day, *The Andy Griffith Show* seems to be on some channel 24/7. I imagine kids today still know who Opie is. Although not in his older brother's league, Clint had a successful career as a child actor as well.

Ron describes his father as both "thrifty and handy," two good things for a father of sons to be. Without a father in the home, boys will learn to be neither. A man who can fix things is a valued commodity everywhere, even in Hollywood. That skill grounds a man, gives him a sense of worth and competence. He will keep his wife happy and never want for work, even if just around the house.

During the first read-through of the premiere episode of the show, Rance read the lines for Ron, who had not yet learned to read. As written, Rance noticed that the Opie character came off as a little wiseacre "smarter than his father." Even in 1960, this inversion of the right order was becoming standard sitcom fare. Although wary of seeming like the aggressive stage dad, Rance screwed up his courage and approached Andy Griffith. "Ronny can get laughs doing these kinds of lines, I get it," said Rance. "But wouldn't it be more interesting and unusual if Opie actually respected his father?"[19]

Andy could have blown Rance off. Opie was not yet a star. Rance would never be. And Andy already was. But Andy saw the wisdom in Rance's suggestion. Both "country boys," they had similar worldviews and similar values. Ron only learned of this conversation years later, and he learned of it from Andy. His father never mentioned it. As Andy told Ron, he directed his writers to model the Andy-Opie relationship on the Rance-Ronny one. "Out of this talk came a crucial creative decision," writes Ron, "that helped chart the course of a tremendously successful, era-defining show."

Reflecting back on his father's role, Ron marveled at how he decided to sacrifice his own career as an actor for his son's. He attributed his father's ability to adapt without fuss or self-pity to his "midwestern Zen," the ability to deal with what life handed him and soldier on. "He chose to be a great parent—to support his children's opportunities with everything he had. His responsibility, and therefore his priority, became me, and, a little later, Clint."[20] Unusual for Hollywood, Rance and Jean stayed together until her death nearly fifty years after their marriage. Ron, a successful director and producer, emulated his parents' model. He and his wife, Cheryl, have four children and will soon be celebrating their fiftieth wedding anniversary.

NFL great Ben Watson and his wife, Kirsten, have seven children, and much of what Watson knows about fatherhood, he learned from his own father. In my interview with Watson, he tells of how as a boy of nine or ten, he went with his dad to a Toys "R" Us.[21] His father made a purchase, paid the cashier, and looked at the receipt only on the way to the car.

"She gave me too much change," his dad said to Ben. The first thought that went through Ben's mind was, "Great. Let's get out of here." But that's not what his father thought.

"Gotta go make this right," he said to his befuddled son, explaining that the cashier might have had to make up the difference herself at the end of the day. So saying, he went back to return the change. "You always do what is right,

Benjamin," said his dad. "You always do what's right." That is a lesson Watson never forgot.

Dr. Lauren Miller extrapolated Ben's experience to society writ large. A boy needs a role model to show him "how to make good decisions, how to show restraint, how to de-escalate from conflict." Miller explains that these "are not innate skills. These are things children need to be exposed to, need to learn, need to practice." In the absence of a father or a good substitute, boys will learn their values somewhere else, and that somewhere is rarely wholesome. The loss of a father has a "domino effect," says Miller. Worst case, that loss "affects the entire community."

My Fox News colleague Sean Hannity boils the things a father should teach his son down to four "rules." Hannity, who is my mentor, treats me as something of a second son. The rules that he has shared with his own son he has shared with me. First and foremost is the Golden Rule—in Jesus's words (Matthew 22:37–39), "You shall love the Lord your God with all your heart, with all your soul, and with all your mind" and "You shall love your neighbor as yourself." The second rule is less lofty but more direct: "Drugs will destroy your life. Don't do them. Ever." The third rule has some wiggle room to it: Drinking has its place but "don't be the idiot kid throwing up in the bushes." And the fourth rule is second only to the first in importance: "Revere women and put them on a pedestal."[22]

Before leaving this subject, I should add a cautionary word about the male's role as protector. In the course of my reporting with Fox News, I have had the honor of getting to spend time with some of America's best and bravest, the men who comprise what are called "Tier One Special Mission Units."

These units—Delta Force, Navy Seal Team 6, and Army Rangers Regimental Reconnaissance most notably—serve as the tip of America's spear. To a large degree, love of country motivates them to risk their lives in its service. Equally important, however, is their strongly felt need to protect their own families. If we don't do it, they tell me, who will?

In a sense, any responsible man serves as the tip of his own family's spear. A woman provides essential support, but it is the man whose essential duty it is to protect his loved ones from harm. This role can take an emotional toll. More than a few of the Tier One men with whom I met suffer a letdown when the adrenaline ebbs. This is when PTSD can affect the psyche, as can the soul-shattering moral injuries front-line troops almost inevitably sustain.

Tough as these guys are, they need support from time to time. We all do. One way we can grow as men is to acknowledge we are not invulnerable. Men do need to be babied or want to be, but if we are to be the protectors that God intended us to be, we have to do a better job of understanding how we feel and sharing those feelings with significant others in our lives, male and female.

CHAPTER 3

The Godly Man

You may not have heard the word "presentism," but you have probably met more than a few people who practice it. The official definition of presentism is "uncritical adherence to present-day attitudes, especially the tendency to interpret past events in terms of modern values and concepts."[1] As you know, those who preach this gospel usually add a dose of courage to their résumé. You will hear them say things like, "Well, if I were in Nazi Germany, I would have resisted," or, "If I were with Columbus, I never would have tolerated the abuse of the natives."

Not so fast. The "presentists," if I can call them that, have little understanding of where the truly heroic figures in the

American past got their courage. If you told them the source was their faith in God and usually their faith in Jesus Christ, they would scoff. The presentists of my acquaintance tend to think of Christianity as part of the problem. No, the real problem is that presentists don't understand their history, let alone their Bible.

Many would suggest that God has no place in the quest for manhood, that the idea of God is somehow outdated. I would disagree. As Jesus said, recorded in John 14:6, "I am the way, the truth, and the life. No one comes to the Father except through Me." From my perspective, to be a Godly man is to accept that challenge. Institutions of all sorts have rules and regulations, but without the Holy Spirit guiding us, we are just going through the motions. We are living a life without ultimate purpose, and that ultimate purpose should be pleasing God, not ourselves. Jesus died on the cross to redeem us. Following in His path is the least we can do to honor that sacrifice.

If anyone doubts the need for God in our lives, even among the strongest men, all you would have to do is watch the spontaneous response among the football players who witnessed the near-fatal collapse of Buffalo Bills safety Damar Hamlin. Putting all rivalry aside, nearly all of the Bills and the Bengals knelt in collective prayer in midfield. Bills quarterback Josh Allen called the moment a "spiritual awakening."

"To see what's transpired here, it's a crazy, crazy feeling," said Allen. "It's something I've never felt before. It's something I know a lot of my teammates have never felt before. You can't really do anything but accept it and lean on your brothers and share that moment with them."[2] At the beginning of Super Bowl LVII, both opposing quarterbacks, Patrick Mahomes and Jalen Hurts, quietly and independently took a knee to pray. Not too long ago, quarterback Tim Tebow was mocked for doing the same thing.

I do not intend to preach here. I am in no position to. Although I aspire to be a Godly man, I cannot deny my own very human weaknesses, which is why I turn to God for guidance. My own father played a major role in setting me on a righteous path. In 2008, I was all in for Barack Obama. In fact, I was a precinct captain at fifteen. Although my mother is a minister, my father is more of a searcher. For years he avoided religious institutions, in large part because he was skeptical of their business practices. Then he began to listen to Tony Evans, the senior pastor of the Oak Cliff Bible Fellowship in Dallas. Given my interest in politics at the time, my father recommended that I hear out Evans as well, especially on the subject of government. I am glad I did.

"At the heart of the American idea is freedom," says Evans.[3] This understanding of freedom derives from the very first government. That is the compact between Adam and Eve and God, a compact based squarely on freedom. God gave them a bounteous Garden to cultivate and enjoy freely as their hearts saw fit, but with freedom came responsibility. The one responsibility they had was to honor a single restriction—not to eat the fruit from the tree of the knowledge of good and evil.

What that tree represented was the supremacy of human reason. To eat from it was to cast aside divine revelation under the assumption that man was wiser than God. This is a powerful temptation. Humans have been seduced by their own imagined wisdom since the beginning of time.

As example, Evans cites the First Book of Samuel 8:18, in which the people of Israel, having escaped Egypt, forsake God and clamor for an earthly king. Samuel tells the people what will happen if they get their way: The king will draft their children into service, seize their property, and divide it among his cronies. Once this has come to pass, "And you will cry out in that day because of your king whom you have chosen for yourselves, and the Lord will not hear you in that day." The people of Israel were no more inclined to listen to a cautioning voice than were the followers of Lenin or Mao or Pol Pot when promised an earthly paradise. Like those who followed their example in future centuries, the Israelites paid the price for their vanity.

Evans argues that the role of government is to assure a "safe, just, righteous, and compassionately responsible environment for freedom to flourish." Freedom always comes with restrictions, but those restrictions should flow freely and naturally from God's law. He rejects laws that are arbitrary, unnatural, and needlessly restrictive.

Upon introducing me to Evans's wisdom, my father asked me straight out whether the "values" promoted by Barack Obama and the Democratic Party were in alignment with divine revelation. Of course, I was not about to admit that they were out of alignment, but the more I studied Evans and learned about God's role in the formation of America, the more I saw just how out of whack were the values of a political party that embraced "choice" only when it involved the killing of the unborn. My evolution had begun.

The Bible, I came to see, is very clear in what it expects from men, but living as we do in an age of skepticism, many of us are reluctant to commit to Godly virtues or to admit it if we do. I believe, however, that if a male is to engage the world, he must, as Evans insists, "promote the will of God in history through civil government."

Looking at our history through a fresh lens, I began to see how God's hand has helped shape it. Abraham Lincoln makes for an interesting case study. As a young man, like many young men, he questioned just about everything, including faith. He never did align himself with any one sect, and unlike some modern politicians, he never made a show of religiosity. His natural reserve led some to wonder whether Lincoln was an agnostic or even an atheist. Historians who cherry-pick his writings try to make that case. Serious historians know otherwise. The mature Lincoln was a man of deep and growing faith and a useful role model for us all.

In winning the presidency in 1860, Abraham Lincoln assumed more responsibility than any man should ever have to shoulder. His election all but guaranteed that Southern states would begin peeling away from the Union. Their secession from the Union all but guaranteed that war would follow.

In the South, millions of those enslaved looked to Lincoln as a potential liberator. In the North, thousands of abolitionists looked at Lincoln skeptically, wondering whether he would have the nerve to liberate those enslaved. Everywhere Lincoln turned, there were enemies, some among them

potential assassins. Even among his friends, there were doubt-
ers. If any man ever faced a test of his manhood, it was Lincoln when he assumed office in March 1861.

By December 1860, South Carolina had seceded from
the Union. In January 1861, Mississippi, Florida, Alabama,
Georgia, Louisiana, and Texas followed suit. A week after
Lincoln's inauguration, Southern delegates in Montgomery, Alabama, approved the Constitution of the Confederate
States of America. A month later, Confederate forces opened
fire on Fort Sumter in South Carolina. Three days after Fort
Sumter, Lincoln issued a public declaration proclaiming that
a real insurrection existed. In the declaration, he called for
an armed response to stop the rebellion. This call for volunteers led Virginia, Arkansas, North Carolina, and Tennessee
to secede from the Union in the weeks that followed. Lincoln
had the shortest and most brutal "honeymoon" in American
political history.

Lincoln, however, had a resource about which few knew.
Unknown to his enemies and even to some of his friends, Lincoln had become what the Reverend Evans calls a "Kingdom
man," that is, "a male who places himself underneath God's
rulership and lives his life submitted to the lordship of Jesus
Christ."[4] Although he shied from using the name "Jesus,"
Lincoln talked often of the "savior," more often as his faith
matured. Had he not opened his heart to the "Lord," another
word he uses with frequency, the whole history of America
would have been different and not in a good way.

There is ample proof of the same. Upon leaving Springfield, Illinois, for the nation's capital as president-elect,

Lincoln made a heartfelt plea for the prayers of his friends as he faced "a task before me greater than that which rested upon Washington." In a stop at Columbus, Ohio, Lincoln turned for support "to the American people and to that God who has never forsaken them."[5] With the onset of war and the death of his beloved son Willie, Lincoln's faith grew deeper still.

In a proclamation for a national day of fasting and prayer, Lincoln made his sympathies abundantly clear. "It is the duty of nations as well as of men to own their dependence upon the overruling power of God," he wrote, "and to confess their sins and transgressions in humble sorrow, yet with assured hope that genuine repentance will lead to mercy and pardon, and to recognize the sublime truth, announced in Holy Scripture, and proven by all history, that those nations only are blessed whose God is the Lord."[6]

Throughout his presidency, Lincoln shows a humility before God that is heartfelt and essential. In a proclamation from March 1863, he implores his fellow citizens "to humble ourselves before the offended power, to confess our national sins and to pray for clemency and forgiveness." He also believed that prayer mattered. He sent a message after the Battle of Gettysburg to General Dan Sickles telling him that he had gotten down on his knees and prayed for victory. "I cannot explain it," wrote Lincoln, "but soon a sweet comfort crept into my soul. The feeling came that God had taken the whole business into His own hands and that things would go right at Gettysburg and that is why I had no fears about you."[7]

On March 4, 1865, just a month before war's end and his own death, Lincoln delivered his second inaugural address. If any other president gave a speech more indebted to the spirit of the Bible, I do not know what it is. The concluding paragraph has justly become part of our national lore.

> With malice toward none; with charity for all; with firmness in the right, as God gives us to see the right, let us strive on to finish the work we are in; to bind up the nation's wounds; to care for him who shall have borne the battle, and for his widow, and his orphan—to do all which may achieve and cherish a just and lasting peace, among ourselves, and with all nations.[8]

In other countries, victors do not give speeches like this. Here Lincoln promises a civil government that provides what Evans sees as the ideal, namely a "safe, just, righteous, and compassionately responsible environment for freedom to flourish."[9] Certainly, at the conclusion of World War II, Stalin made no reference to any of these virtues in declaring victory over Germany with its "wolfish habits." No one would have taken Stalin seriously if he had. He had, after all, approved the plundering of Germany and the raping of its women. He gave all glory to "our heroic Red Army" and to "our great people, the victor people."[10] In the Soviet Union, the leadership had no need for God, and God, history suggests, finally had no need for the Soviet Union.

As Lincoln knew, he was building on the legacy of the people who came before him. In England, the devoutly Christian political leader William Wilberforce almost single-handedly inspired Britain to end the slave trade. If slavery had existed from almost the beginning of time, abolitionism was a new phenomenon altogether, and no one was more responsible for its development than Wilberforce. "If there is no passionate love for Christ at the center of everything," said Wilberforce, "we will only jingle and jangle our way across the world, merely making a noise as we go."[11]

The movement on both sides of the Atlantic was Christ-driven. Wilberforce faced ridicule for the depth of his faith. Among the political classes, religious zeal was thought as unbecoming as it is today in American universities. Abolitionists in America faced considerably more danger, however, because slavery was so significant a part of the economy. To brave the dangers they faced, American abolitionists, almost to a person, pulled their strength from their faith. Perhaps the boldest of our abolitionists was William Lloyd Garrison, a "Kingdom man" to the core. Born in 1805, a generation later than Wilberforce, Garrison was among the first in America to demand "immediate and complete emancipation of all slaves." So saying, he provoked lethal hatred among that class of people whose economic well-being depended on the presumed ownership of captive people.

Garrison's immediate problem was not the slaveholders. In 1831, in the inaugural issue of his publication, *The Liberator*, Garrison made clear that he "found contempt more bitter, opposition more active, detraction more relentless, prejudice more stubborn, and apathy more frozen" in New England than he did in the South. Like truth tellers to this day, Garrison threatened the complacency of his fellow citizens, their self-satisfaction, their contentment with the status quo. Pro-life activists understand the sentiment completely.

Then as now, self-described "moderates" liked to think themselves paragons of wisdom and restraint. Garrison had no use for them. "On this subject," he wrote of slavery, "I do not wish to think, or to speak, or write, with moderation...I am in earnest—I will not equivocate—I will not excuse—I will not retreat a single inch—AND I WILL BE HEARD." Heard he was. He was also imprisoned, bullied, beaten, and even had a fatwa placed on his head by the state of Georgia. For all the peril he faced, Garrison remained as undaunted as the Apostle Paul and for the same reason. He understood the source of his courage. "I will go forward in the strength of the Lord of Hosts—in the name of Truth—and under the banner of Right. As it is not by might nor by power, but by the Spirit of God, that great moral changes are effected."[12]

In August 1841, Garrison attended an anti-slavery meeting in Nantucket, and there he met a young man who would help change the world. His name was Frederick Douglass. Urged to speak about his experiences as a slave, the hesitant Douglass gave a talk that riveted Garrison and the others in attendance. "I think I never hated slavery so intensely as at that moment," wrote Garrison. "Certainly, my perception of the enormous outrage which is inflicted by it, on the godlike nature of its victims, was rendered far more clear than ever."[13]

Like Garrison, Douglass was a Kingdom man. While an adolescent in Baltimore, he thought himself "a poor, broken-hearted mourner, traveling through the darkness and misery of doubts and fears." Like so many men before and after, he "finally found that change of heart which comes by 'casting all one's care' upon God, and by having faith in Jesus Christ, as the Redeemer, Friend, and Savior of those who diligently seek Him."[14]

Douglass needed all the help he could get. In the American experience, no institution has been more hostile to manhood than slavery. Although a slave owner himself, Thomas Jefferson was among the first to acknowledge that slavery corroded the virtue of both "master" and "slave." (Although neither of these words accurately describes the true status of either, for historical reasons—and simplicity's sake—I will use both of these words going forward.)

"There must doubtless be an unhappy influence on the manners of our people produced by the existence of slavery among us," Jefferson wrote in his *Notes on the State of Virginia*. "The whole commerce between master and slave is a perpetual exercise of the most boisterous passions, the most unremitting despotism on the one part, and degrading submissions on the other."[15] For all his great achievements, Jefferson's role in this institution prevented him from becoming the man he might have been—and he knew it. One limitation was a lack of faith. A nominal Christian—he preferred the label "deist"—Jefferson put his faith in reason. On the subject of slavery, reason could not provide the courage he needed to protest publicly.

As Douglass would be the first to admit, he caught some breaks early in his life that gave him more perspective on slavery than those who knew nothing else. Those "breaks" did not include knowing his father, reportedly a White man, or having any regular contact with his mother even when she was alive. Soon after her death when Douglass was about seven, he was sent to live with a family in Baltimore to take care of their young son. He had no regrets about leaving the plantation behind. Nothing was holding him there.

Baltimore surprised Douglass, not just for its size and its relative grandeur, but for the nature of at least some of the White people who lived there. "And here I saw what I had never seen before," writes Douglass of his new mistress, Sophia Auld. "It was a white face beaming with the most kindly emotions." So deprived was he of decent human interaction that his encounter with Sophia brightened up his life "with the light of happiness."[16] So used was he to groveling before Whites that he scarcely knew how to react when Sophia looked him in the eye and spoke to him as a real human being.

This happy state of affairs did not last long. Before things went awry, however, Sophia started to teach Douglass how to spell. When her husband found out, he went ballistic. Teaching Douglass how to read and write, he scolded Sophia, "would forever unfit him to be a slave. He would at once become unmanageable, and of no value to his master." Not only would knowledge make him useless as a slave, Mr. Auld insisted, "It would make him discontented and unhappy."[17]

Even as a boy, Douglass understood instinctively that Auld knew what he was talking about. Douglass writes, "The very decided manner with which he spoke, and strove to impress his wife with the evil consequences of giving me instruction, served to convince me that he was deeply sensible of the truths he was uttering." Knowledge would, in fact, make Douglass one very discontented and potentially dangerous slave. Knowledge was power. "I now understood what had been to me a most perplexing difficulty—to wit, the white man's power to enslave the black man."[18]

Douglass had heard the word "abolition" before, but Whites on the plantation inevitably used the word as a pejorative. "If a slave ran away and succeeded in getting clear, or if a slave killed his master, set fire to a barn, or did any thing very wrong in the mind of a slaveholder," he observes wryly, "it was spoken of as the fruit of abolition."[19]

As inspired as he was by the abolitionist literature, reading it made him "abhor and detest" his enslavers. He notes, "That very discontentment which Master Hugh had predicted would follow my learning to read had already come to torment and sting my soul to unutterable anguish."[20]

Then as now, for all the power that knowledge brings, it is a burden to know what is wrong with society and not have the means to fix it. For Douglass, that burden was particularly heavy as he dared not even express his thoughts except to those he absolutely trusted. "The slaveholders have been known to send in spies among their slaves," he writes, "to ascertain their views and feelings in regard to their condition."[21] To protest that condition was to risk physical punishment or banishment to some miserable plantation in the Deep South.

After seven eventful years in Baltimore, Douglass, now about fourteen, was sent back to the plantation where he had spent his childhood. "Master Thomas," the man who now dictated the terms of Douglass's life, showed the corrosive power of slave-owning in its purest form. As Douglass implicitly understood, one could not be "inhumane" and still be a man worthy of respect. Inhumanity subverted all attempts at manliness. Douglass had hoped that Thomas's seeming religious conversion would make him less cruel. As Douglass would have known, a genuine acceptance of God into one's heart has the power to redeem a lost soul. He loved "the pure, peaceable, and impartial Christianity of Christ."

He knew the history of the Apostle Paul well enough to know how God's grace can transform the cruelest of tormentors into the most compassionate and fearless of men, one capable of enduring being stoned, beaten, and shipwrecked in order to spread a message of love and charity.

Master Thomas was no Paul. Like many slave owners, he cherry-picked the Bible for verses that seemed to justify his abusive ways. As Douglass saw things, Thomas's alleged conversion "neither made him to be humane to his slaves, nor to emancipate them. If it had any effect on his character, it made him more cruel and hateful in all his ways."[22] Douglass, like Garrison, made no bones about his contempt for the hypocrisy of those who called themselves Christian and yet condoned slavery. Going to church did not begin to make one Godly.

One day, watching the sailboats glide up and down Chesapeake Bay, Douglass had something of an epiphany. Their very freedom of movement reminded him of his lack of the same. "O God, save me!" he cried out. "God, deliver me! Let me be free!" Prayer may help, he understood, but God helps those who help themselves. "I have only one life to lose," he reflected. "I had as well be killed running as die standing."[23] For Douglass, this resolution represented a giant step into manhood.

Douglass did eventually escape and made his way to Connecticut with his new wife, Anna. There he found what might seem unglamorous work loading oil onto a ship, but he went at it "with a glad heart and a willing hand." The reason was simple: "I was now my own master." In explaining the satisfaction that comes with a job freely entered into, Douglass observes, "I was at work for myself and newly-married wife." He calls this new responsibility "the starting-point of a new existence."[24] He has moved into a new stage of manhood that slavery denied the young male, the direct responsibility for his own family.

As Tony Evans observes, God "holds the man responsible for the condition of the home." Under slavery, this was not possible. "What does it look like for a husband to model his love for his wife based on Christ's love for His church?" Evans asks. "First, Christ gave up His life to deliver His church from sin and death and to save her for a relationship with Him."[25]

Today, unfortunately, the welfare state imposes many of the same obstacles as slavery did on the male-female relationship. If one natural impulse is to escape a life of brutal enslavement, another is to indulge in a life of subsidized irresponsibility. Whether enslaved by outside forces or seduced by them, the result is often the same: the failure of the boy to become a man. As a free man in the libertarian nineteenth century, Douglass never had the luxury of not working.

Before the war's end, Douglass had a chance to meet with President Lincoln. He was awed by the improbability of it all. "I was an ex-slave, identified with a despised race," Douglass writes, "and yet I was to meet the most exalted person in this great republic." Douglass's mission was to urge the president to assure that enlisting Black soldiers were treated the same as White ones. Douglass was more than a little apprehensive about the meeting. He did not need to be. Lincoln immediately put him at his ease.

"I at once felt myself in the presence of an honest man— one whom I could love, honor, and trust without reserve or doubt," writes Douglass. As he proceeded to tell Lincoln who he was, Lincoln stopped him, saying, "I know who you are, Mr. Douglass."[26] I can only begin to imagine how Douglass must have felt. To be greeted by a president even today in such a fashion would be heart-stopping.

On one point of discussion, Lincoln's schooling in Biblical doctrine shone through. Douglass wanted the Union generals to retaliate in kind against the unlawful murder of Black prisoners by Southern forces. Lincoln rejected the idea, arguing that "hanging men for a crime perpetrated by others was revolting to his feelings." Although Douglass disagreed with Lincoln on this point, he respected his "humane spirit."[27] It is easy to forget how unusual Lincoln's restraint was. The history of warfare, right up and through the present, is a history of retaliation, often mass retaliation, against innocent parties. America, though, had a higher percentage of Biblically literate citizens than any nation in the world. As cruel as the Civil War could be, soldiers on both sides showed a level of respect for civilians, women especially, unmatched in world history. For the Union, Lincoln set the example.

Garrison also met with Lincoln before the end of the war. An idealist like Douglass, Garrison had been a frequent critic of Lincoln's pragmatism. By June 1864, when the two men met at the White House, Garrison had come to a fresh understanding of the president's wisdom. "Mr. President," said Garrison, "from the hour that you issued the Emancipation Proclamation, and showed your purpose to stand by it, I have given you my hearty support and confidence."[28] Like Douglass, Garrison endorsed Lincoln for president in 1864, something neither had done in 1860.

Despite their strategic differences, each of these three brave men worked tirelessly for the same cause, and all looked to the same source of inspiration for the courage to soldier on. Said Garrison of *The Liberator* when shutting it down at the end of 1865, no publication "has gone beyond it in asserting the Fatherhood of God and the brotherhood of man."[29] As all three heroes understood, the brotherhood of man derived from the fatherhood of God.

One hundred years after the death of Abraham Lincoln, President Lyndon Johnson signed the Voting Rights Act into law. It took a long century to complete the process, but America had finally extended the promise inherent in the founding documents to all of its citizens. This time, too, it was courageous Godly men who had pushed the nation across the finish line.

Secularists would like us to forget the prominent role that men of faith, Christians and Jews, played in the Civil Rights Movement. A half century after the passage of the Voting Rights Act, *Time* Magazine editorialist Mary Eberstadt said out loud what every thinking person knew to be true. "This new vigorous secularism has catapulted mockery of Christianity and other forms of religious traditionalism into the mainstream," wrote Eberstadt, "and set a new low for what counts as civil criticism of people's most-cherished beliefs. In some precincts, the 'faith of our fathers' is controversial as never before."[30]

Although I am a huge Douglass fan—I have his image tattooed on my right arm—I was once among those secularists who resisted God's call. I trace that resistance to my involvement with the Democratic Party and my adolescent hero worship of Barack Obama.

Today's most prominent inheritors of the Civil Rights Movement, the activists of Black Lives Matter, show little interest in the source of that movement's strength. "Because of its thoughtfully-crafted agenda, values and mission, BLM is unmistakably incompatible with Biblical Christianity," writes Meeke Addison in the prominent evangelical journal *Decision*. Addison, who is herself Black, draws her conclusion about the organization's Marxist founders from the BLM website. Although professing solidarity with their Christian sisters, they do little to prove their sincerity. "While these women may care about injustice and racism," adds Addison, "they also care about normalizing sexual deviance, deconstructing the Biblical definition of family, and strong, black men who identify as straight."[31]

"Black Lives Matter," writes Mark Levin in his bestseller *American Marxism*, "is a product of the fusion of Marxism and CRT." Levin is talking here more about the organization than the movement. In the movement are many people who are simply advocating for civil rights and equal justice. The organization is another thing altogether. Funded almost exclusively by affluent white liberals, it works against many of the core values of the Black community.

On the BLM board are "trained Marxists with a history of extremism and violence." Levin sees BLM as part of a larger coalition hell-bent on destroying the family first and ultimately the nation. One part of a man's role as a protector, he tells me, is to counterprogram his children and grandchildren. "The more you know," says Levin, "the less likely you are to be indoctrinated. When you study history, you can make better judgments about what you are seeing and hearing."

The major civil rights leaders of the last two hundred years—Malcolm X, Frederick Douglass, W. E. B. Du Bois, Booker T. Washington, the Reverend Martin Luther King Jr.—would not have aligned themselves with BLM's mission. The three women who founded BLM are free to be whoever they want to be—lesbians, Marxists, or both. And of course Black lives matter. We can all agree to that, but the BLM founders have set out to destroy the historic Christian, patriarchal roots of the Black experience, and that does no one any good.

King and his colleagues at the Southern Christian Leadership Conference would have rejected BLM's values, such as they are, without hesitation. Although by no means perfect, these were Kingdom men to a person. In 1955, the twenty-six-year-old King, a third-generation Baptist pastor, led the groundbreaking Montgomery bus boycott. For the next thirteen years, he would lead one nonviolent protest after another until his assassination in 1968.

In 1963, King was arrested by Birmingham police after leading a demonstration in that deeply segregated and often violent Alabama city. In longhand, from the Birmingham jail, he wrote a memorable letter to some sympathetic, if timid, White Southern pastors who questioned the need for an Atlanta activist to lead a public protest in a state other than his own.[32]

King understood better than the pastors the source of his inspiration. "Just as the Apostle Paul left his little village of Tarsus and carried the gospel of Jesus Christ to practically every hamlet and city of the Greco-Roman world," he reminded the pastors, "I too am compelled to carry the gospel of freedom beyond my particular hometown."

There was nothing rash or irresponsible about the nature of the protest King led. He described for the pastors the four steps he and his colleagues took before going public with their protest. These included a review of the perceived injustice, an attempt at negotiation, self-purification, and direct action. The self-purification involved a series of workshops on nonviolence in which volunteers would have to prove their capacity to withstand abuse and even imprisonment. Only then, writes King, would we "present our very bodies as a means of laying our case before the conscience of the local and national community."

Slowly and imperfectly, the national community responded. Reverend Evans defines freedom as "the unimpeded opportunity and responsibility to choose, to righteously and justly and legally pursue one's divinely created reason for being."[33] The work of men like Lincoln, Garrison, Douglass, and King created the opportunity, but it will take many more Kingdom men to help realize that opportunity for all.

As Ben Watson has learned, not all Godly causes have been exhausted. When his first child was born in 2009, he and his wife, Kirsten, became acquainted with the wonders of ultrasound technology. Seeing their child in the womb gave them both a new appreciation of life. So inspired was Kirsten that she encouraged Ben to begin buying ultrasound technology for crisis pregnancy centers. The couple bought five of them.

Watson was more than comfortable with the turn his life was taking. He learned the Biblical worldview at home as a child and believed that "womb to tomb, people matter." He understood, too, that abortion affects Black babies disproportionately. He also understood, of course, that championing the pro-life cause would win him few friends in media newsrooms or NFL boardrooms.

Although he never made a conscious effort to become a pro-life spokesman, "God used my passion for life and justice." In 2017, Watson spoke at the annual March for Life, an event attended by several hundred thousand people. "It happened," he tells me, "and I'm walking in the light trying to be faithful." It is the same light that has guided many great Kingdom men before him.

CHAPTER 4

The Disciplined Man

My dad had a rule: If we forgot one dish when we were washing up after dinner, we'd have to wash every single dish all over again. That rule instilled discipline in us from an early age and taught us the importance of having order and structure in our lives. A parent doesn't have to be harsh, but being firm helps kids grow within appropriate limits. Providing accountability and not accepting excuses prepares kids for the harsh reality of the real world.

Boys especially need a firm hand. A longitudinal study of ten thousand Australian boys and girls over the first nine years of their lives showed boys, on average, displaying a higher rate of behavioral problems at every stage of development. On average, too, mothers express less competence in managing their sons than their daughters.[1] The data from America vary little from Australia's. The bottom line is universal: Boys and girls are different. For a boy to become a man, a father or a father figure must help make him one.

It helps society considerably when institutions reinforce the discipline that children, especially sons, learn at home. The sports world has a mixed record on this score. Kansas City Chiefs head football coach Andy Reid, who has served as a father to five and father figure to many more, knows better than most that discipline is a complex issue.

In his twenty-four seasons as a head coach, first with the Philadelphia Eagles and then with the Chiefs, Reid has been among the most successful coaches in the National Football League. He has had only three losing seasons and taken both the Eagles and the Chiefs to the Super Bowl, winning with the Chiefs twice. Unlike many winning head coaches, Reid has led his team more with love than with fear. "I can't remember anyone who didn't like playing for him, and I can't imagine why anyone wouldn't like playing for him," Geoff Schwartz, a former Chiefs offensive lineman, told ESPN. "He's everything you want in a coach."[2]

Schwartz played for the Chiefs in 2013, Reid's first year with the team. Reid warned the team that training camp would be tough, and it was, but said Schwartz, "The things he told us, he did for us." Former linebacker Derrick Johnson agreed, "We trusted him right from the start. Andy is a straight shooter. He did everything he told us he would do. That's what everybody loved." Reid is known for creating a harmonious team culture. Critical to sustaining that culture is a coach's ability to let go of players, even stars, especially stars that choose not to adapt.

Wide receiver Tyreek Hill overcame some serious off-the-field issues to become a superstar with the Chiefs. In 2014, as a student at Oklahoma State University, he was arrested for domestic abuse against his pregnant girlfriend, Crystal Epinal. Oklahoma State expelled him. Hill pled guilty and avoided prison, and the Chiefs subsequently drafted him in 2016. After three successful seasons with the Chiefs, Hill came under suspicion once again, this time when his and Epinal's three-year-old son suffered a broken arm.[3]

A local TV station aired a recording of Hill explaining his style of parental discipline. "You do use a belt. That's sad," said Hill. "Even my mama says you use a belt." When Epinal said their son was "terrified" of Hill, he responded, "You need to be terrified of me too, bitch."[4] After an initial suspension from the Chiefs and the NFL, Hill was allowed to return because "the NFL cannot conclude that Mr. Hill violated the Personal Conduct Policy." It helps to be a superstar. The Chiefs rewarded him for dodging this bullet with a $45 million, three-year contract extension. The money would help Hill pay for his additional three children born in 2019, twins with Epinal and a son born to another girlfriend.

In 2022, however, when Hill held out for more than the Chiefs were willing to pay him, the Chiefs cut their losses and traded Hill to the Miami Dolphins. In Hill's case, his own lack of internal discipline is not hard to understand. Born to two teenage parents, Hill was raised by his mother. When the biological dad split, his mother's father stepped in to help discipline the boy. He was not the ideal grandfather.

Reportedly, he physically abused his grandson when not committing crimes of his own. By the time Hill signed with the Chiefs, his grandfather had been involved in fifteen criminal cases and was convicted at least four times.

Hill may mean well. He has a tattoo on his chest that reads *He Strengthens Me* and one on his neck that says *Forgive Me*. As the Reverend Tony Evans reminds us, however, we can enjoy the freedoms that God gave us only if we recognize that freedom has its boundaries. Evans, in fact, uses football as an analogy to remind us that we can succeed only if we play between the lines. Instead of nurturing Hill's better angels, however, the NFL has repeatedly appeased his inner demons. Its coaches and executives have cut Hill more slack than they would a player on the margins. With a net worth of some $40 million, Hill has learned that he can buy or cajole his way out of jams that would have sidelined a lesser mortal.

Unlike Hill, Andy Reid's two sons, Garrett and Britt, grew up with a loving father, but love was apparently not enough. As well intentioned as Reid was, there are few jobs that consume as much of a man's time and focus as that of a head coach in the NFL. Discipline demands more than good intentions. As Dr. Lauren Miller reminds us, "Time spent is the greatest gift a father can give a child."

In 2013, at ESPN's request, Baltimore Ravens head coach John Harbaugh documented a workweek as his team prepared for a November game at Chicago. "There's always more you could do," Harbaugh told ESPN. "But if you don't sleep, you can't function." Harbaugh's week began with a Monday wake-up at 5:00 to 5:30 a.m. "on the office couch." He allotted fifteen minutes that morning for a phone call with his wife and a half-hour lunch with his wife and ten-year-old daughter.

The rest of the day was dedicated to meetings, news conferences, game reviews, a workout, a dinner with assistant coaches, and bedtime on the office couch at 11:30 p.m. "Sleeping at the office is about maximizing my time," Harbaugh told ESPN. "I can get more done if I eliminate time I'd spend driving home. Plus, if I come home too late, chances are I'll wake up my wife." On some nights, he drove home but usually no earlier than 10 p.m. On Friday evening, he allotted a few hours to play with his daughter.

On Saturday morning, Harbaugh was back at work by 7 a.m. and off to Chicago that afternoon. After the game on Sunday, he flew home, his mind racing. "It's tough," he said. "You know how much everyone put into that game, but the clock is already ticking. You've got to come up with what you're going to install next week, and you only have a few days to do it." At 12 a.m. on Sunday night, he returned home once again and kissed his wife good night. The next week would be more of the same.[5]

At some point in the future, Reid might write a memoir in an effort to make sense of the unfortunate paths his sons followed, but in the interim, we can only extrapolate from the facts on the ground. Before proceeding, I'd like to remind readers that I am not a father myself, and I am in no position to cast judgment on anyone involved. I write this story only as a cautionary tale and aim it especially at those who think love can compensate for the absence of consistent discipline. It cannot.

By all accounts, Andy Reid tried to be as good a father as he was a coach. As an assistant coach with Green Bay, Reid would arrive at work at 4 a.m. so he could return home to see his kids off to school. Small-town living made that possible. In 1999, Reid took a job with the Philadelphia Eagles. The family bought a home in suburban Villanova a good half-hour drive from the team's facilities in South Philadelphia. At the time of the move, Garrett and Britt were in their early teens, an awkward time to move in the best of circumstances. Their dad tried his best. Eagles president Joe Banner says of Reid, "He was as loving and caring a father that I have ever seen."

As adolescents growing up in suburban Philadelphia, Reid's sons had everything a father could provide except for his time. The year 2007 found them both living at home. Garrett was twenty-three, Britt twenty-one. Incredibly, on the same January day, both were arrested on felony charges in unrelated incidents. Garrett, high on heroin, ran a red light in his SUV and crashed into a car, injuring a woman. Britt pointed a handgun at another motorist in a road rage incident. Reid took his sons to Florida to enroll in a drug rehabilitation program, but Britt was arrested again for drunk driving and drug possession while awaiting adjudication of the road rage incident.[6]

At the sentencing of the two young men in November 2007, a Pennsylvania judge lectured Reid and his wife. "You've got to take accountability of what goes on in the house," said the judge, calling their home "a drug emporium." He sentenced both young men to prison for up to twenty-three months. Unlike with Hill, Reid could not just cut his losses.

He promised to get his sons all the help they needed, but at this stage, medical help wasn't the answer.

In 2012, Garrett died of an accidental heroin overdose. In 2020, Britt, now an assistant coach under his father, had another road rage incident. According to a police report, Britt assaulted the motorist, an off-duty police officer, and lied to the police about his involvement. The local district attorney chose not to press charges against the son of the coach of the reigning Super Bowl champs. Three months later, and three days before Kansas City's next Super Bowl appearance, Britt drove away from the team's practice facility drunk. At a high speed, he rammed his truck into a disabled car, leaving a five-year-old girl in that car permanently brain damaged.

The Chiefs did not renew Britt's coaching contract, but the prosecution went soft on Britt once again, allowing him to plea to a three-year prison sentence. A local defense attorney explained the lenient sentencing to the *New York Times*. "The prosecutor had all the cards and could prove his case," said the attorney. "Maybe it was because he was Andy Reid's son, maybe there was a little bit of politics behind the scenes."

Discipline begins in the home, but it doesn't end there. When the institutions in our society turn a blind eye to the misdeeds of those deemed special, they undermine what little discipline these young men learned at home. These boys never become men, and the community suffers.

The early years of Supreme Court Justice Clarence Thomas were unlike those of the Reid sons but very much like those of fellow Georgia native Tyreek Hill. Although a good athlete, Thomas did not have the special talents that allowed Hill to live above the law. More importantly, he had an omnipresent grandfather who enforced the law in his own home.

As with Hill, Thomas's father quickly disappeared from his life, and his beleaguered single mom turned the boy over to her father to raise. Myers Anderson, a name very few recognize, was the man Thomas called "Daddy" to the very end of Anderson's life. "In every way that counts, I am my grandfather's son," writes Thomas in his soul-piercing memoir of that same name, *My Grandfather's Son*. "He was dark, strong, proud, and determined to mold me in his image."[7]

Before proceeding, I should note that Clarence Thomas has a complicated relationship with the Black community, females in particular. To stop his nomination in its tracks, the powers that be in Washington pitted him against a Black woman, Anita Hill. That he had a White wife by his side seemed to confirm some people's suspicions.

To a degree, all Black conservatives are distrusted by those within the Black community who judge one's "blackness" by the degree of their loyalty to the Democratic Party. Having been a community activist since I was an adolescent, I have surer footing in the Black community than some of my conservative brethren. That said, I understand the distrust, especially toward conservatives like Clarence Thomas who seem remote and unengaged.

It is hard for Black America to believe someone like Thomas loves them when they don't see him. It's even harder for them to receive his ideas when they feel he is speaking at them and not locking arms with them, even though his end goals may be the same as theirs. I would encourage skeptics to read what follows. Having reviewed Thomas's history and his highly principled tenure on the Supreme Court, I think he deserves the fair hearing he did not get thirty years ago.

Thomas endured his most memorable trial by fire, the Supreme Court confirmation process, in 1991, a year before I was born in December 1992. What I know of that ordeal is what I have read in books and seen in documentary films and heard about through the grapevine. I can only imagine what it was like to experience in person, especially to be the lone man at the center of that unimaginably furious storm.

I can also only imagine what it was like to grow up where and when Thomas did. Being Black gives me some insight into his experience but not that much. Thomas spent his early years in a speck of a town called Pin Point, Georgia. A midwife came to the shanty where his mother lived and delivered him at home in June 1948. Of course, there was no air-conditioning. No heat either. There wasn't even a bathroom, at least not indoors. A single light bulb served up the only electricity in the house.

The shanty was located on a sandy, heavily wooded peninsula ten miles south of Savannah. Although Jim Crow was still the order of the day in the South, Thomas did not feel its sting as a young boy as there were no White people in Pin Point. In fact, just about everyone who lived in this isolated town at water's edge was related to him. For adults, life was hard. Most men pulled an unpredictable living from the sea. But for Thomas and his younger brother, Myers, life was simple, uncomplicated, even "idyllic." He had no idea of the greater world beyond.

I was born into that greater world, specifically in Garland, Texas, a Dallas suburb with more people than in Savannah,

Georgia, let alone in Pin Point. Unlike the Pin Point of 1948, Garland is about as diverse as cities come. Today, it has nearly as many Asians as Blacks and as many Hispanics as Blacks and Whites combined.

At age six, Thomas and his brother were ripped from their own little paradise and shipped to Savannah, not the eccentric, tourist Savannah, but the unseen part of the city, "the foulest kind of urban squalor."[8] There, they lived with his mother in a dingy one-room apartment without indoor plumbing. As to his biological father, whom Thomas refers to as "C," he says only, "His involvement in my life had ended with my conception." At age seven, Thomas's life took a turn for the better. Feeling that she could no longer manage two adventurous young boys in the mean streets of Savannah, his mother sent them to live with her parents, "Aunt Tina" and "Daddy," as Thomas came to call them. They lived nearby in Savannah but in better quarters.

What is impressive about Daddy was his self-reliance. He built the home himself out of cinder blocks and painted it a gleaming white. He put in hardwood floors and installed, wonder of wonders for Thomas, an indoor bathroom as well as a separate kitchen, two bedrooms, a dining room, and a den.

What is sometimes lost in the retelling of the Black experience in America, even in the Jim Crow South, was that civil authorities did not deny Black Americans the right to free enterprise. As a boy, Daddy worked on his uncle's boat but then branched off into his own business. He bought an old truck and began selling firewood. He then expanded to coal and ice and eventually fuel oil. He built a few more houses on his own and turned those into rental properties. Internal discipline is essential for entrepreneurial success. With no one telling you what you must do every day, you have to tell yourself.

No doubt his world was unjustly constricted by the customs of the Old South, but nowhere else in the world in the mid-twentieth century did an ordinary working man expect to have his own vehicle or to run his own business free from the interference of the state. Historically, American males of all ethnicities lived with the expectation—and the burden—that they would provide for their families and, to the degree possible, manage their own lives. This was the path to American manhood.

Unfortunately, the state has chosen over the years to pave that path, not with gold, not even with promises of gold, but with the guarantee of mere subsistence. These guarantees have undercut marriage and manhood in a thousand different ways. Daddy knew this instinctively. He told his grandson that accepting welfare would lead to the "ruination" of Black people, given the way it undermined the male's desire to work and provide for his family. As his career advanced, Thomas saw nothing to dispute Daddy's wisdom, and the ruination was hardly limited to Blacks.

Having no other children at home, Daddy and Aunt Tina accepted the boys into their home under the condition they stay there until adulthood. On the morning Thomas and his brother moved into their grandparents' home, Daddy let them know, "The damn vacation is over." Their days as wild street kids were in the past. They were about to begin the domestic equivalent of boot camp. There would be rules and regulations but also expectations. "The first rule," writes Thomas, "was that Aunt Tina was always right—and so was Daddy."[9] During his early life, Thomas often questioned Daddy's dictates, but the older he got, the more he began to see the good sense embedded in that hard-earned wisdom.

I find myself identifying with Thomas, less because we are both Black than because his relationship with Daddy so mirrors my relationship with my own father. Given the upward mobility implicit in being American, many young males find ourselves with more formal education than the men who raised us. Many of us, me included, have convinced ourselves— at least for a while—that we are smarter than these men. Wisdom comes with the understanding that we are not.

I suspect that readers of all races can read a little bit of themselves into the father-son dynamic in the Anderson household. Dean Cain certainly could. He tells of coming home one night as a young teen an hour past curfew with alcohol on his breath. His father met him on the street, and every third step he took, "My father kicked me in the ass." Dean adds a useful qualifier, "There was love between the kicks. I think." Of course there was. Dean knows it. Love is the variable that separates discipline from abuse.

In the South, even during my own childhood, there was plenty of love and plenty of discipline, and the latter often took physical forms. My own dad was not one to spare the rod. "A hard head makes a soft behind," he would tell us. When my brother and I got too big to spank, he would make us do squats while holding heavy books in our hands. If we read the books, we would make our burden lighter.

Given my background, I followed closely the child abuse accusations against star NFL running back Adrian Peterson, a fellow Texan. In 2014, he was indicted for using a "switch" on his misbehaving four-year-old son. A switch, Peterson explained, was just a narrow tree branch. As a child, his parents had taken a switch to him on a regular basis. Millions of other Southern boys from time immemorial knew the drill. The greatest sin in many a household was to disrespect your elders. I am not in a position to judge whether he had crossed the line into abuse—only the courts can do that—but my father, who could get physical, was never abusive.

I suspect we may be worse off as a society for abandoning the switch in favor of, say, "time out." Just in the years since I was a kid, disrespect toward our elders seems to have become epidemic. Dean Cain blames the current plague "on the lack of strong male figures in kids' lives."

Clarence Thomas knew about hard heads and soft behinds as well. "Daddy didn't whip us regularly," he writes, "but our encounters with his belt or a switch were far from infrequent."[10] Like most of the people in his environment, Daddy and Aunt Tina were seriously Christian, but unlike his peers, Daddy had converted to Catholicism. He liked the order and discipline of the Catholic Church and saw to it that Thomas and his brother attended Catholic schools through high school. Given the time and place, the schools were segregated, but the good Sisters taught the Thomas boys that "God made all men equal, that blacks were inherently equal to whites, and that segregation was wrong."[11] It was an important lesson.

Daddy liked the fact that the Sisters were strict disciplinarians much as he was. When they saw fit, they did not hesitate to use corporal punishment. Neither did Daddy. He felt free to use his belt or a switch when the occasion demanded. Although Thomas never felt abused, he expresses some ambivalence about the practice. In that era, throughout America, corporal punishment was an accepted practice.

The fact that corporal punishment of children is taboo in some circles has not stopped irresponsible males from applying it, all too often with a vengeance. Study after study has shown that the real culprit in these abuse cases is rarely the married father of a child, nor even the stepfather, but the mother's boyfriend with an emphasis on "boy." A congressionally mandated National Incidence Study showed that unrelated males in the home are eleven times more likely to abuse the children in their charge than are the children's biological fathers.[12] We will explore this problem in more detail later, but the numbers show the tragic consequences of raising up a generation of males content to remain "boyfriends."

Although he would later indulge Thomas's son Jamal with tenderness and affection, Daddy was called by a sense of duty to stay hard on his grandsons. For them, he was the responsible party. If he did not assume the role of disciplinarian, no one would. Thomas may have chafed under Daddy's guidance, but he learned a lot in the process, especially during the summer. When Thomas was about eight, Daddy decided to build a house on an uncultivated sixty-acre property that had been in the family for generations. He enlisted his reluctant grandsons in the construction project.

For the next ten years, Thomas spent every summer day working on the farm. Years later, Daddy explained to his grandson that he built the house as a way to keep Thomas and his brother off the Savannah streets. Thomas describes that farm as "a place of torment—and salvation."[13] The torment was the obvious part. From sunup to suppertime, with a break for breakfast and lunch, Thomas and his brother did hard, hands-on work under the heat of a Georgia sun—clearing land, cutting trees, building fences, plowing the fields, weeding, picking beans. After supper, the chores were easier, but they were chores still—clearing the table, doing the dishes, feeding the animals.

The work helped Thomas understand the relationship between input and output, work and results. You plant in the spring, harvest in the fall. You shoot game, you skin it and clean it. You raise a chicken, you kill it, pluck it, prepare it. Life is hard. Rewards are hard earned. Because of man's fall from grace in the Garden, Daddy reminded his grandsons, it was their lot in life to work "from sun to sun." There was no better way perhaps to acquire wisdom, a prerequisite for becoming a man. Daddy had little use for those "educated fools with no damn sense," and he wanted to make sure his grandsons did not join their ranks.[14]

Daddy never let his grandsons wear work gloves. He thought them a sign of weakness. Thomas came to see the absence of work gloves as a metaphor for life. After a few days of hard, constant work, his hands blistered. After a few weeks, the bloody blisters changed to calluses that protected the hands from pain. Writes Thomas, "Blisters come before calluses, vulnerability before maturity."[15]

Life in the city under Daddy's guidance was not much easier. In addition to school, Thomas spent Saturdays and evenings driving around in Daddy's unheated truck helping him deliver heating oil. "The family farm and our unheated oil truck became my most important classrooms," Thomas writes, "the schools in which Daddy passed on the wisdom he had acquired in the course of a long life as an ill-educated, modestly successful black man in the Deep South."[16]

Thomas would take the lessons learned in Daddy's classroom and apply them to the world beyond. That world was changing by the day, and without those lessons, Thomas would never have been able to navigate it successfully. If America was in transition and its values under attack, the virtues that defined a man were timeless and unchanging. The very word "virtue" derives from the Latin *vir*, meaning "man," and its derivative *virtutem*, meaning "force, strength, vigor; moral strength; qualities, abilities."

Thomas attended a Catholic grade school whose nuns understood that boys and girls were different. Unlike today, the school library was stocked with books written for boys aspiring to be men. Writes Thomas, "I spent countless hours immersed in the seafaring adventures of Captain Horatio Hornblower, the gridiron exploits of Crazy Legs McBain, and the real-life triumphs of Bob Hayes, the world's fastest man."[17]

The book series featuring Royal Navy officer Hornblower is set during the Napoleonic Wars, a century and a half before Thomas was born and several thousand miles away. British author C. S. Forester had written a dozen of the books in this series by the time Thomas was old enough to read. Today, these books would be dismissed as irrelevant, even offensive in that they celebrate Great Britain during its imperialist age.

Critics, of course, are almost surely unaware that the British Navy sacrificed uncountable wealth and thousands of lives in the nineteenth century to end the African slave trade. At the time, Thomas would not have been aware of that sacrifice either, but in Horatio Hornblower, he saw a man like the man he hoped to be—a man of humble birth who overcame his outsider status and his many, almost crippling anxieties to become admiral.

Except for one lost period in his life, Thomas has relied on God for direction. In fact, at sixteen he enrolled in a seminary near Savannah to finish out his high school education. For Thomas, this was his first venture into the White world, and his success at that school persuaded him that he could compete in any environment. After leaving the seminary, Thomas gained entry into the College of the Holy Cross in Massachusetts. He also entered what he called the "angry Black man" period of his life. He threw off his faith in God and faith in America. Freed from Daddy's financial assistance, Thomas felt free to separate himself emotionally and intellectually. "He'd never heard of Hegel, Kierkegaard, or Marx," writes Thomas, "so I wrote him off as an ignorant illiterate incapable of understanding or facing the facts about racism."[18] For his part, Daddy could not understand how a college student could deceive himself into feeling oppressed.

Despite his alienation from Daddy, Thomas never lost the sense of internal discipline Daddy had drilled into him. That self-direction saw him through Holy Cross and then Yale Law School. After Yale, Thomas meandered, torn between a life of public service and a need to make money to pay off his student loans. His relationship with Daddy remained uneasy during this period.

Intellectually, Thomas had begun to shed the radical orthodoxy he absorbed on campus and to move to the right. His thinking on subjects like race and welfare more and more mirrored what Daddy had been telling him all his life about public assistance. It "takes away your manhood," Daddy reminded him. Once an individual accepts government handouts, he insisted, "They can ask you questions about your life that are none of their business. They can come into your house when they want to, and they can tell you who else can come and go in your house."[19] Thomas remains a champion of individual rights.

In 1983, not long after Thomas was appointed to head the Equal Employment Opportunity Commission under President Ronald Reagan, Daddy suffered a stroke while working in the fields and died on the way to the hospital. Although overwhelmed with grief, Thomas took solace knowing that he and Daddy had reconciled shortly before his death. They had come to see that the friction between them derived from the fact that they were so very much alike. They had embraced for the very first time in their lives. A few weeks later, Aunt Tina suffered a stroke and died as well. Without Daddy, she had lost the will to live. As Jesus reminded us, husband and wife "are no longer two but one flesh."

At the EEOC, Thomas found his footing, and his star began to rise. Just as importantly, he met and married Virginia, the soul mate he had always been looking for. The son from his first marriage, Jamal, came to live with them, as did his six-year-old great-nephew, Mark Martin. Perhaps even more important than his renewed creation of family was his return to the faith he shared with Daddy. "Each morning I stopped at a Catholic church on my way to work and asked God for 'the wisdom to know what is right and the courage to do it,'" Thomas writes. "It was one more giant step toward home."[20]

"By running away from God, I had thrown away the most important part of my grandparents' legacy. Now I began to reclaim it, bit by bit," Thomas says. He forced himself to admit that these "unsophisticated, ill-educated people…understood all along what I was only just beginning to accept, but grief is a great teacher. While I still had a long, hard road to travel before I would be fully ready to re-embrace my lost faith, the pilgrimage had begun in earnest."[21]

I tell this story here not in judgment—who am I to judge?—but in wonder. Few case histories document the road to manhood more vividly, and in recent American history, no man has been put to the test more publicly and dramatically than Clarence Thomas was in the fall of 1991. I study this story in awe and admiration. It remains one of the great American sagas.

Most readers of a certain age will know it well. I will summarize it quickly for those who do not. At the heart of the story is abortion. In 1973, on the flimsiest of constitutional pretexts, the U.S. Supreme Court yielded to the passions of the day and justified legal abortion as a "right to privacy" found deep in the various "penumbras" of the U.S. Constitution.[22] With the election of Ronald Reagan in 1980 and the appointment of "originalists" to the Supreme Court, pro-abortion forces mobilized to block the appointment of judges who respected the Constitution. They succeeded with the brutal takedown of the esteemed Robert Bork in 1987 and were prepared to do the same when President George H. W. Bush appointed Thomas in 1991.

Only forty-three at the time of his nomination, Thomas was a double threat. As a young man, he could be a conservative force on the bench for thirty years or more. As a Black man, he sent a message to young Black Americans that they could, as Thomas did, "reject the ideological orthodoxy that was prescribed for blacks by liberal whites."[23] When it seemed likely Thomas would pass Senate review on the merits, leftist activists tried one last desperate gambit. Those who watched the Brett Kavanaugh hearings got to see a replay, but the original was even uglier.

The fact that Thomas was Black made it so. The left's accusations played to all the worst stereotypes of the Black man in America. His accuser, Anita Hill, was Black as well, but she, too, was a Yale Law grad and a member in good standing of the feminist elite. As was true with Christine Blasey Ford a generation later, Hill made for a compelling witness. Her charges against Thomas were as questionable as Ford's, but she presented them with enough conviction to be believable. The media mobilized around her. As with Ford years later, journalists chose to believe Hill without questioning her account. They were all in for abortion's survival and Thomas's defeat.

To defeat him meant they had to forever stain his reputation. Thomas would not stand for that. "I didn't care whether I ever sat on the Supreme Court," Thomas writes, "but I wasn't going to let what little my family and I had cobbled together be so wantonly smashed."[24] After Hill, egged on by the committee's liberal senators, aired her various demeaning charges against the nominee, Thomas insisted that he have his say. It was no longer about strategy or talking points. It was about standing up like a man and speaking out from the heart.

I would recommend that anyone who has never seen Thomas in action do so today. Upon watching his appearance before the Senate Judiciary Committee on YouTube, I marvel at how he was able to discipline the passion raging within and make his case before the world. Here is what he said to the shocked Democrat senators, committee chair Joe Biden most directly, and to millions of Americans glued to their TV sets:

> The Supreme Court is not worth it. No job is worth it. I am not here for that. I am here for my name, my family, my life, and my integrity. I think something is dreadfully wrong with this country, when any person, any person in this free country would be subjected to this. This is not a closed room. There was an FBI investigation. This is not an opportunity to talk about difficult matters privately or in a closed environment. This is a circus. It is a national disgrace. And from my standpoint, as a black American, as far as I am concerned, it is a high-tech lynching for uppity blacks who in any way deign to think for themselves, to do for themselves, to have different ideas, and it is a message that, unless you kowtow to an old order, this is what will happen to you, you will be lynched, destroyed, caricatured by a committee of the U.S. Senate rather than hung from a tree.[25]

Democrats weren't used to being spoken to like that. Despite the fact that their party fought to keep slavery alive, started the Ku Klux Klan, instituted Jim Crow, and resisted its demise, they somehow convinced themselves that they were the saviors of Black America. Thomas had the scars to prove otherwise. Those who watched the hearings overwhelmingly supported Thomas. The pressure the public brought to bear convinced just enough Democrats and wobbly Republicans to confirm his nomination.

Owning the media as they did, the liberal elite would rewrite history and make a heroine out of Anita Hill, or at least try to. With less success, they would try to do the same with Christine Blasey Ford. Both efforts were in vain. Their worst fears were realized in 2022 when Kavanaugh and four other justices joined Thomas in overthrowing the unconstitutional reign of *Roe v. Wade.*

On a more personal level, Thomas showed to the world and proved to himself what a man can and should do when under pressure. He never forgot who taught him. "I'd always been able to look to Daddy as a living example of strength and fortitude," Thomas writes. "At one of our last meetings, I'd complained to him about how badly I was being treated because of my views. 'Son, you have to stand up for what you believe in,' he said. It was just that simple, for it was just what Daddy had done his whole life."[26]

CHAPTER 5

The Chivalrous Man

At six-foot-five, I have no trouble putting a suitcase in the overhead rack on an airplane. I learned this kind of common courtesy from both my mother and my father. They taught me that I should offer to help anyone, male or female, who was struggling with a suitcase or anything else. In Texas, this is expected behavior. So is offering women compliments and, yes, putting them on something of a pedestal.

On one occasion, I boarded an Amtrak in New York heading for DC. I did this often enough that the waiter knew what I wanted. "The usual?" he asked. After a frantic week, a Jack and Coke sounded perfect. Then I looked up and saw sitting across the aisle from me, traveling by herself, none other than the actress Cicely Tyson. At the time, Ms. Tyson was in her nineties, but as a younger woman, she helped open the Hollywood doors for people of color. She was still royalty in the Black community, in no small part because of her refusal to play any role that demeaned Black women.

Having absorbed my father's lessons, I decided not to have a drink. I needed to stay sharp in case Ms. Tyson needed anything. Once I gathered up my nerve, I approached and asked if there was anything I could do for her. She smiled and said with her natural elegance, "I'm just fine, baby." Cicely Tyson understood where I was coming from. She died in 2021 at the age of ninety-six. Her comment still warms my heart. "Baby"—I like that.

When I first moved to New York, I found that not all women got me the way Ms. Tyson did. Some women today, I learned, do not want to be helped and resent the very offer of assistance. The message they are getting from feminist media is that if chivalry is not dead, it ought to be. I beg to differ. A man should treat everyone he meets with courtesy and respect, especially women.

The word "chivalry" has its roots in the French word "chevalier," meaning "horseman." The practice of chivalry developed as a way to rein in the behavior of medieval knights whose very business was warfare. Scholars trace the chivalrous codes to the *Song of Roland*, a twelfth-century French poem celebrating a French victory over the Moors in Spain some three centuries earlier. Those codes included the following vows[1]:

Fear God and His Church
Serve the liege Lord in valor and faith

Protect the weak and defenseless
Live by honor and for glory
Respect the honor of women

Man, we all know, is a fallen creature. War unfortunately is part of our nature. What the chivalric codes attempted to do was to remind the warriors that God sees all and stands in judgment. The codes also made a very specific point of respecting the honor of women. A millennium ago this was a radical notion, one that needed to be taught and reinforced. Building on the Jewish tradition, Christians honored women in a way few other cultures did, if any. 1 Peter 3:7 reminds us, "Husbands, likewise, dwell with *them* with understanding, giving honor to the wife, as to the weaker vessel, and as *being* heirs together of the grace of life, that your prayers may not be hindered."

Feminists may take issue with the word "weaker," but in an era when virtually all work was manual, there was no overlooking the obvious physical differences between men and women. Men were taller and stronger, and strength mattered more than it does today. But rather than exploiting women, given their relative weakness, the chivalric codes demanded that men respect women. Dean Cain, who personified chivalry in his role as Superman, nicely sums up its spirit. "However strong you may be," he tells me, "the ability to humble yourself before God and say yes there's a higher power—that is why I do the things I do." Cain adds, "That's why I'm kind when I don't want to be kind."

To be sure, not all knights honored these codes, but their celebration in romantic literature from medieval times until now has helped remind even the warriors among us that women share equally in God's grace.

In the early nineteenth century, chivalry had no greater champion than Scottish novelist and poet Sir Walter Scott. His works proved so popular in the United States that his detractors accuse him of having provoked the American Civil War. In a *New York Times* article titled "The Author of the Civil War," historian Cynthia Wachtell writes, "Sir Walter Scott, more than any other writer, shaped Americans' conception of manliness, bravery and combat in the period leading up to the Civil War." In his day, Mark Twain went even further: "Sir Walter Scott had so large a hand in making Southern character, as it existed before the war, that he is in great measure responsible for the war."[2]

What critics of chivalry, then and now, refuse to consider is the effect that chivalry had on restraining and refining male behavior. Feminist-influenced historians, in particular, struggle to come to terms with the treatment of females in the Civil War. "Historians will sometimes consider the American Civil War to be an anomaly among other wars," writes author Annika Jensen grudgingly, "because they claim the adversaries did not use widespread sexual violence as a battle tactic."[3] The Civil War *was* an anomaly in this regard. Both sides discouraged sexual violence and punished rapists.

In fact, Scott sold more books in the North than he did in the South, but it wasn't Scott who tempered behavior. It was the fact that America was a deeply Christian nation. Of course, most Southerners and more than a few Northerners carved out an exception to their faith to support slavery just as today many American Christians carve out an exception to support abortion, but a Christian respect for women was deeply ingrained in the national culture.

In one of the war's more controversial incidents, William Quantrill and his irregular band of Southern sympathizers launched a surprise raid on the sleeping town of Lawrence, Kansas. Legend has it that Quantrill, just twenty-six at the time, stopped on a hill overlooking the town, pointed to a tree, and threatened to hang from it any man who so much as touched a woman. The results suggest that there may be truth to that legend. Some 150 men and adolescent boys were killed, but not a single woman was molested, let alone killed. In the twentieth century, the women of Nanjing and eastern Germany would have welcomed just a hint of chivalry from the invading armies. Unguided by a Christian God and encouraged by their own leaders, Russian and Japanese soldiers raped literally millions of women as a matter of policy.

In 1912, the ocean liner *Titanic* struck an iceberg and put the concept of chivalry to the test. For a variety of reasons, critics have tried to debunk the notion that men, particularly the men in first class, behaved gallantly as the ship sank. Hollywood producers, in particular, like to play at Marxism. Despite their wealth and power, they imagine themselves on the same side of the barricades as the little guy. As a case in point, James Cameron, the director of the 1997 blockbuster film *Titanic*, portrayed as the villain of the piece an affluent American male whose behavior was cowardly to the point of parody.

In real life, the men in first class were mostly British or American, and they honored the chivalric codes they had grown up learning. The numbers don't lie. Women and children did get preferential treatment. Nearly 75 percent of the females survived the disaster, but only 20 percent of the men did. A higher percentage of women in third class survived than did men in first class.[4] The passengers and crew who stayed on board reportedly sang "Nearer, My God, to Thee" as they watched their loved ones flee to safety.

In January 2009, nearly a century after the sinking of the *Titanic*, a flock of birds put the "women and children first" dictum to the test. When those birds caused two of the engines of US Airways Flight 1549 to catch on fire, Captain Chesley "Sully" Sullenberger ditched the plane in the Hudson River. Amid the ensuing chaos, wrote Thomas Maugh in the *Los Angeles Times*, "Sullenberger was firmly in control and his edict that women and children should exit first was followed, even though the plane was in imminent danger of sinking."[5] Miraculously, everyone survived.

Some accounts of this near tragedy question whether all the passengers complied with the edict, but no article that I could find questioned the logic of Sully's order, despite its apparent "sexism." In the *Times* piece, Maugh cited University of Michigan psychologist Daniel Kruger, who argued that people instinctively aspire "to save those who have higher reproductive value, namely the young and women in child-bearing years." This may be so, but this chivalric "instinct" needs to be reinforced by the culture if it is to endure.

Missouri Senator Josh Hawley was reminded of the culture's fragility when he made a pitch for chivalry at the 2022 Turning Point USA conference. "Young men, let me make a suggestion to you," Hawley said to the youthful crowd. "Why don't you turn off the computer, and log off the porn and go ask a real woman on a date." Hawley was addressing a phenomenon older adults may not even know exists—the involuntarily celibate, or "incel," movement. As Lyman Stone of the Institute for Family Studies observes, the movement comprises mostly young men "who feel shut out of any possibility for romance, and have formed a community based around mourning their celibacy, supporting each other, and, in some cases, stoking a culture of impotent bitterness and rage at the wider world."[6]

Hawley addressed a problem his critics refused to acknowledge. "How about that? Just a thought," he continued. "Show her a little respect. And you take her out and you treat her right…treat her like what she is, a woman, a person of incredible significance created in the image of God. And you know what, you treat her right and then one day you do her the honor and show her respect of asking her to marry you."[7]

Hawley's talk shocked the gawkers on social media. One reason to read their comments is to see how repetitive and uninspired they are. The males who responded, almost to a person, attacked Hawley's masculinity. Programmed to object to Hawley on political grounds, female critics refused to recognize the female-friendly content of what he said. "This seems even creepier coming from a US senator," said Jeanne. Tweeted Suki, "Treat her right by taking away her most basic right." Added Roberta, "Like he would know what a real woman is lol. Besides, what's wrong with a little porn?" Slygrammy repeated the one word that showed up most often in the responses, namely "creepy" and its derivatives, "This guy puts out the creepiest vibes."[8]

Sean Hannity has instructed his own son—and me as well—in the everyday application of the chivalrous spirit: Whether the girl wants you to or not, you open the door; you always pay for dinner or whatever entertainment you have asked her to; you put her on a pedestal and keep her there; you never raise your voice; and if the relationship is going nowhere, be man enough to end it graciously. I took notes!

Despite efforts to ridicule the spirit of chivalry, it lives on. Scarcely a day goes by that we don't see an example of it in the news. A 2022 story out of Sacramento tells how a "good Samaritan" traveling down the highway with his young daughter stopped and rescued a woman trapped inside a burning car.[9] The newscaster may not have known how perfect the "good Samaritan" reference was, and I suspect many Californians could not even begin to trace the reference to its source, namely the Bible.

As a reminder, in Luke 10 we hear the parable that Jesus shared with a legal expert to reinforce the principle to love "your neighbor as yourself." In the parable, a man is robbed, beaten, stripped of his clothes, and left to die on the side of the road. First a priest and then a Levite, on seeing the man, crossed the road to avoid helping him, and they were presumably of the same ethnicity as the victim. The Samaritan was a foreigner, a distrusted "other." He had no tribal obligation to the man, but he stopped to help him and went to great lengths to save his life.

"So which of these three do you think was neighbor to him who fell among the thieves?" Jesus asked the legal expert.

"He who showed mercy on him," he replied.

"Go and do likewise."

The road in this case was Interstate 80. The good Samaritan was a young Black man named Elton Ward. The person needing help was an older White woman named Kristine Smith, partially disabled by recent knee surgery. The fire department arrived minutes after Ward risked his life to pull Smith from a car that exploded seconds later. A department spokesman acknowledged that Smith would likely have died were it not for Ward's intervention.

When asked why he did what he did, Ward answered, "We all got grandmas, grandpas, little nieces and nephews, brothers whatever. If you all see my people, I want you to try to help my people. So that's somebody's people." Ward captures here the essence of Christ's Golden Rule, which is at the core of the chivalric code.

Said Smith to Ward when they reunited, "You became my grandson that day." She understood, too, why this all happened. "Thank the Good Lord he sent me a good Samaritan that stopped for me," she told the reporter. "I think that it all comes back. The community needs to have more young people and more examples like this."

As it happens, when I asked NFL vet Ben Watson to give me an example of a "man," he cited the good Samaritan. "That's a man," he said. "He is strong enough in his own identity to be open enough to do something countercultural." There was no incentive for him to help someone of a different tribe other than that internal voice calling to him, "This is what a real man does."

I do not know much about Elton Ward, but I do know he was ready for the moment. The spirit of chivalry had not been educated out of him. Nor do I know much about Kristine

Smith, but I do know she understood and appreciated that spirit. All young men should be as mentally prepared as Ward was, and all women should be as grateful for the help as was Smith. To throw this relationship into doubt is nuts. The synergy is as natural as it is God given.

Women play a critical role in sustaining this synergy. In St. Augustine, Florida, not long ago, a woman named Kelly, her fourteen-year-old son, Ty, and a thirteen-year-old friend of the family, Gia, got caught in a vicious riptide. When Kelly realized how desperate the situation was, she instructed Ty to save Gia, and that he did. Kelly was on the verge of drowning when a "heavy-set, hairy-chested balding man about average height" plunged into the water in an attempt to save her.[10]

When the stranger, gasping desperately for air, pulled Kelly up on the beach, two nurses who just happened to be nearby started emergency CPR on Kelly. Her lips had already turned blue, and she surely would have died had it not been for the two female nurses and the male stranger who pulled her from the sea. Not needing any glory, the stranger just wandered back into the anonymous life of a heavyset, hairy-chested, balding man about average height. He, too, was ready for his moment, as was the fourteen-year-old Ty, who rescued his female friend.

The small, slight, fifty-two-year-old Sean Conaboy was ready for his moment as well. Few stories capture the larger themes of chivalry as well as his does. Conaboy was standing on a New York City subway platform when he caught the dead eyes of a strange young man who seemed up to no good. Conaboy's suspicions proved correct. Out of nowhere the young man, twenty-two-year-old Joshua Nazario, grabbed the fifty-four-year-old Kelli Daley from behind and started stabbing her. When Daley screamed for help, Conaboy did not waste a second. He rushed past the other subway riders, tackled Nazario, and held him, now with the help of some bystanders, until the police arrived, saving Daley's life. "It was the only thing to do," said Conaboy.

The Diocese of Brooklyn agreed. In an emotional ceremony, Bishop Nicholas DiMarzio honored Conaboy, a devout Catholic, with a medal inscribed, *Verbum caro factum est*, the Latin for "The word became flesh." Bishop DiMarzio explained that Conaboy had put his faith into practice, doing exactly what a good Christian is expected to do under those circumstances. "You gave help to someone in trouble, did not concern about your own safety, and we really tip our hat to you," said the bishop. Bishop Kevin Sweeney added, "While I was surprised to see him being interviewed, I wasn't surprised because he was someone I knew as a person of faith."

For his part, Conaboy recognized that his actions were guided by a divine force. He was at that particular subway platform only because the train he usually took wasn't running. "Some angel or saint had been watching over me, for sure," he told a reporter. "Because I really, at one point or another, thought that my whole back is exposed, I have no ability to see anything."[11]

Conaboy had the grace and the courage to overcome his fears. I hope otherwise, but I suspect that he may be one of a vanishing breed. Consider, for instance, what happened on a public transit train in Philadelphia in October 2021. Before any number of eyewitnesses, according to police, thirty-five-year-old Fiston Ngoy harassed a woman on a train for forty minutes before sexually assaulting her, and none of the other passengers intervened. A year later, he pled guilty as charged.[12]

This story resonated internationally but especially among public transit riders. All the regular transit passengers interviewed by local media reacted in shock on hearing the story. "Ridiculous," said one woman. "Disgusting," said another. "Awful," said a third woman, asking, "What's wrong with people?" One woman added a thought with which no sane person would disagree, "If we were in that position, we would want someone to help."[13] Exactly. "I believe in being chivalrous 100 percent," Mark Levin tells me. "My wife expects it from me." Most wives do. Levin argues that men should school themselves to intervene whenever they see a woman being abused, even if at a risk to themselves. That way they will be mentally prepared to act if they should see an incident like the assault in Philadelphia.

When interviewed by NBC News, psychologist Bibb Latané attributed the passivity of the victim's fellow passengers to what he calls "the bystander effect." Said Latané, "When people are in public, they are less likely to show their concern about something than if they are alone. And what that means is that…when they see other people aren't yet doing anything, they may be led to think that 'well, maybe there's no reason to do anything.'"

Here, Latané does what too many experts do, especially when discussing young men. They attribute the failure to act like a man to some disorder or other, if not the "bystander effect," then ADD or ADHD or PTSD or some other condition. In so doing, they absolve males of responsibility for their own behavior and trivialize the plight of those who actually do suffer from some crippling anxiety like PTSD.

I wish the Philadelphia incident was a one-off, but it's not. I see videos almost daily of passive male bystanders doing nothing other than pulling out their cell phones and recording an incident in which a woman is attacked or harassed. I don't know how they live with themselves. I would like to think that the guilt weighs heavily on their hearts, but I wonder sometimes if the guilt has been trained out of them.

That's a shame all around. As the female transit riders interviewed in Philadelphia made clear, they want men to behave like men. They even expect them to and are disappointed when they don't. Yet many people in our media and education establishments, women especially, mock the very idea of chivalry. Their message trickles down. Every time a woman snickers at a male who holds a door open or picks up a check or helps her with her luggage, she increases the risk level for herself and other women. Young males no longer know how to behave. They may even fear a scolding if they offer assistance, even to a woman in peril.

Schools unfortunately provide little guidance for young males in their journey to become men. I have reviewed school reading lists in vain looking for books that show men in action battling evildoers or the elements to save their family or their nation. The all-too-typical Baldwin Arts and Academics Magnet School in affluent (and influential) Montgomery County, Maryland, recommends six books for incoming eighth graders.[14] Four are written by females. Of the two written by males, one is a romance. The other is a novella, *The*

Pearl, by Nobel Prize–winning American author John Steinbeck. *The Pearl* does at least deal with a young man's attempt to provide for his family and defend them, but his obsession with a pearl that he finds leads to the abuse of his wife and the death of his infant son. It is hard to fathom what kind of message an adolescent boy would pull from it.

Absent from just about all school reading lists is any positive reference to God or Christianity. A list from Prestwick House of twenty recommended books for high schoolers is, if anything, anti-Christian.[15] *Bless me, Ultima*, "a classic piece of Chicano literature," deals with "spirituality" but only in a mystical way. *The Hate U Give* "tackles themes of racism, police brutality, and societal injustice." *Unwind* deals with three teens in the aftermath of a second civil war "fought over reproductive rights." I can only imagine. *The Things They Carried* "will educate your students on the horrors of war." *Nickel and Dimed* deals with "the causes and effects of income inequality." *The Poisonwood Bible* tells the story of an arrogant, White, evangelistic minister and his misbegotten effort to bring Christ to the Congo. *The Handmaid's Tale* is Margaret Atwood's absurdly popular novel about a "theocratic regime" in which "women have no autonomy." Feminists convinced themselves that the book somehow reflected life in MAGA America.

Of the twenty books listed, the only one that might interest red-blooded young men is Cormac McCarthy's grim, post-apocalyptic novel, *The Road*. The book, later made into a film, was likely included because readers have interpreted it as a statement on man's destruction of the environment. On the surface, too, it seems to deny the existence of God, especially in lines like, "There is no God and we are his prophets."

On a closer reading, however, this story of a heroic father leading his son to safety—and to manhood—in a world of ashes strikes one Christian theme after another. In the way of evidence, the first words spoken aloud in the book are the father's reflection on his son, "If he is not the word of God, God never spoke."[16]

That said, *The Road* is a difficult read for male high school students, whose willingness to read anything has been eroded by a feminized educational establishment. According to the National Assessment of Educational Progress, by the twelfth grade, the typical boy is a year and a half behind girls in reading. The fact that boys read less than girls is well enough known, but the real reasons why boys read less are either ignored or buried in the literature. A comprehensive article on gender disparity, for instance, notes deep in the text two points that I believe should be prominent[17]:

- Boys tend to resist reading stories about girls, whereas girls do not tend to resist reading stories about boys.
- Boys like to read about hobbies, sports, and things they might do or be interested in doing.

For all the talk of "equity," there is precious little interest in making the small and unobtrusive steps necessary to diminish the gender gap in reading. Of the twenty books recommended by Prestwick House, for instance, not a one deals with sports or adventure, not a one depicts a boy doing something chivalrous or heroic. Several portray young people as victims and, inevitably, white men as the victimizers. Two deal with cancer. One, *The Perks of Being a Wallflower*, is the kind of book only a girl would want to read about a boy, as it deals with "adolescent issues, including social pressures, dating, abuse, and identity." And *The Handmaid's Tale*, seriously? What a dreary lot.

Not that long ago, Disney films dealt with the theme of boys becoming men. The 1994 film *The Lion King* was a roaring success. As a boy, I loved the movie. For a while, I would watch it every single day. It would drive my parents crazy watching me watch it over and over. Careless at the time, I would leave the VCR tape on the floor, and my dad would warn me that one day he would throw it away if I wasn't more responsible.

Of course, like the child I was, I did not listen, and one day the tape just went missing. I was so angry with my father. I accused him of throwing it away. It was something that he, in fact, said he would do. One day, at about age twenty-five, I was having a heated exchange with my father, and he revealed to me what really happened to the tape. I had left it out and he stepped on it, destroying the tape in the process. He preferred that I blame him rather than being upset with myself for leaving it out. I called my mom to verify the story, and she said, yes, she knew all along. It was my dad's way of teaching me a lesson about carelessness and at the same time protecting me from the self-loathing I was still too young to handle.

Like Mufasa, my dad sacrificed himself to save his foolish little Simba. Today, however, Mufasa and Simba belong to an endangered species. In part at least to appease feminist pressure groups, Disney has decided to give many of the more traditionally masculine roles to females. Disney's pitch at the TV Critics Association Winter Press Tour in February 2022 suggests this is a conscious strategy. The Disney presentation generated headlines such as DISNEY AIMS TO EMPOWER NEW GENERATION OF GIRLS IN PROMISING NEW SHOWS, just in time for Women's History Month.[18]

In an article ranking Disney heroines, we learn that Elsa in *Frozen* chooses "to break free of her metaphorical chains and finally live freely." The male characters are incidental to her success. Pocahontas is a "strong protagonist whose penchant for articulated introspection can almost be described as Shakespearean." Esmeralda in *The Hunchback of Notre Dame* "is not afraid to fight for the rights of her people when bigotry and tyranny ravage Paris, nor to assert her bodily autonomy against Frollo's unwanted advances." In *Tangled*, Rapunzel "advances through a compelling, inspirational arc that focuses on her recognizing herself as a victim of abuse and resolving to do something about it."

In *Beauty and the Beast*, Belle "proves that going against the grain is a good thing, especially since her neighbors are simple enough to fall in line with a lunkheaded misogynist like Gaston." The ability of Moana in the movie of the same name to rise above her obstacles "makes her an inspirational figure for young women faced with seemingly insurmountable challenges." Her "aversion to greed and desire for peace, as well as the strength she exhibits in fighting for a better world" makes Raya in *Raya and the Last Dragon* "one of the most honorable protagonists in Disney history."[19] Finally, there is Mulan in the movie of the same name. She "not only demonstrates immense bravery by taking her father's place in the Imperial Chinese Army, but also succeeds at the seemingly impossible task of defeating the Huns."

"People are making these jokes about ours being the PC *Snow White*, where it's like, yeah, it is—because it needed that," said the twenty-one-year-old Rachel Zegler, the half-Colombian star of the live action remake of the Disney classic. "It's an 85-year-old cartoon, and our version is a refreshing story about a young woman who has a function beyond 'Someday My Prince Will Come.'"[20] Yes, of course, what woman—other than perhaps Meghan Markle—needs a prince?

The problem is not so much that Disney is giving heroic roles to females, but that Disney is denying them to males. Mulan, we learn, "builds up her confidence and agility as a warrior, eventually finding a way to bring honor to her family when she never thought she could and remaining grounded all the way."

However improbably, Mulan is the Disney character who best exemplifies the chivalric code and lives out the heroic monomyth. There is no male equivalent in the recent Disney canon. The handsome prince who rescues Sleeping Beauty or Rapunzel or Snow White or Cinderella has been consigned to the dustbin of history. In Disney, it is girls who rescue themselves from "Frollo's unwanted advances" or "a lunkheaded misogynist like Gaston." In real life, however, there are far too few princes riding the Philadelphia transit lines and far too many women unable to rescue themselves. Chivalry has to be learned, and Disney has ceased to teach it.

A Disney subsidiary, the enormously successful Marvel Cinematic Universe (MCU), has been even more consciously destructive of the chivalrous spirit. Its mothership, Marvel Comics, has been churning out superheroes since 1939. Thanks to their representations on TV and in the movies, many of these characters have become household names—Spider-Man, Iron Man, Captain America, Thor, Hulk, and Wolverine among others. Historically, all of these characters have used their superpowers to protect the weak and fight evil. That is why they are known collectively as "superheroes."

As you might expect, fans of the Marvel universe skew young and male and ethnically diverse.[21] Most of the superheroes were specially drawn to encourage young males to identify, if not with them, then with their alter egos. Peter Parker, for instance, is a struggling adolescent until he changes into Spider-Man. Dr. Robert Banner is a weak and insecure physicist until he morphs into the monstrous Hulk. Many of the plots revolve around the character's struggles to channel their strengths to the specific demands of a given problem. The superhero must not only be strong, but he must also be prudent and just.

If I were going to talk about superheroes, it seemed only fitting that I interview one. So I reached out to actor Dean Cain, who played Superman for four years on the popular series *Lois & Clark: The New Adventures of Superman*. As Dean tells me, his life was right out of a *Superboy* comic. Abandoned by his father as a baby, he was adopted by a farmer who, along with Dean's mother, raised him in the South Dakota equivalent of rural Smallville. "Had I not a strong father figure, just like Clark Kent," says Dean, "I would not have learned

these small-town America values—being kind to other people, being strong and stoic, taking on the role of the man."

To Dean's dismay, Marvel has been conspicuously fem-
inizing its characters. Says Dean with regret, "The current
zeitgeist is to emasculate men." In an insightful online video
titled "The Feminization of Your Heroes, Your Stories &
You," its creator R. J. Shaw leads the viewer through a visual
representation of the changes over the years. The highly
knowledgeable Shaw compares the male Marvel fan to the
proverbial frog in the boiling pot of water. The fan scarcely
notices as his characters are incrementally feminized year by
year. The character development, he argues, is anything but
organic. "This is not change," says Shaw. "This is a complete
180."

One commenter on Shaw's site, Patrick Buckley, catches
the drift of the shift in characterization. "The issue is not
feminization, it is emasculation," Buckley writes. "The
removal or demonization of the masculine, and deification of
the feminine." The result, he continues, is the elimination "of
those virtues which once bestowed superheroes with a kind
of mythological majesty."[22]

The Marvel movies are quickly shedding that majesty
as well. In the newest Thor reboot, *Thor: Love and Thunder*, Thor's ex-girlfriend emerges as "the Mighty Thor," fully
able to wield his massive magic hammer. Natalie Portman,
who plays the Mighty Thor, is a petite five-foot-three. Chris
Hemsworth, who plays Thor, is a hulking six-foot-three. The
previous film in the Thor franchise, *Thor: Ragnarok*, netted
an impressive 7.9 fan rating on the Internet Movie Database
(IMDb). *Thor: Love and Thunder* came in at an anemic 6.2.

Other recent superhero movies with female leads, *Captain Marvel* and *Black Widow*, also failed to reach the 7.0 mark, IMDb's minimum level of respectability. On the plus side, none of these films has performed as badly as the absurd *She-Hulk: Attorney at Law* TV series, which registered a woeful 5.2 on IMDb.

These movies do not even succeed in pacifying feminist critics. If anything, they antagonize them. Angelique Nairn, writing for *The Conversation*, objects to the fact that Portman's character, the Mighty Thor, is presented as Thor's girlfriend. "Treating even powerful female characters as subordinate or dependent might reassure male fans that superheroines aren't a threat to the masculine undertones of the genre," Nairn writes, "but it does a disservice to the female audience." The subtitle of Nairn's article reads, "Why it's so hard for Marvel to get its female superheroes right."[23] It's hard because the largely male audience for these films cannot easily identify with female superheroes. The reader is told, by the way, that every article in *The Conversation* "is written by university scholars and researchers." It shows.

In the controversial television series *The Lord of the Rings: The Rings of Power*, Amazon has done more injustice to its source material than even Marvel has done. The series is based on the works of the deeply Catholic British scholar J. R. R. Tolkien. Writing during the troubled years of World War II, Tolkien aimed his books at boys on the cusp of becoming men. In fact, of the four top books on Listopia's "Good Books for Boys Written by Men," three are by Tolkien.[24]

In his *Lord of the Rings* film trilogy produced in the early years of this century, director Peter Jackson respected

Tolkien's material, and the audience rewarded him for it. Of the three films, none has an IMDb rating of less than a stellar 8.8. The films did spectacularly at the box office, and the third film in the series won the Best Picture Oscar. The lead characters in these action-adventure movies are understandably male. As in the subtly Christian-themed Tolkien books, the films highlight the virtues young males will need if they are to embrace free will, resist evil, and become men.

Fast-forward twenty years to the 2022 release of *The Rings of Power*, and the lead character is now the female Galadriel. In the book and in the Jackson film, Galadriel is imagined as a stay-at-home Elf-queen with mystical powers. In *The Rings of Power*, a prequel, Galadriel is "more rebellious, direct, and ambitious," writes one reviewer, adding, "It's no surprise to see *that* version of Galadriel jumping into dirty, steel-to-steel combat, rather than just casting powerful spells during key showdowns."[25] Through its perverse alchemy, Amazon transformed a golden coming-of-age saga for boys into a leaden, improbable mess. The fans at IMDb rewarded *The Rings of Power* with a humbling rating of 6.9.

It did not used to be like this. In its early years, Hollywood presented young men with countless models of men acting bravely and gallantly. The western as a genre emerged as the American equivalent of the chivalric legends. The stranger rides into town and saves women (and men) from outlaws, renegade Indians, snarling banditos, and/or ruthless cattle barons. He then rides out of town with a starstruck boy yelling after him, "Shane, come back." But as the heroic gunslinger tells little Joey in the movie *Shane*, "There's no going back."

Like a wandering knight of yore, Shane moves on after peace has been restored and justice served. "Now you run on home to your mother and you tell her everything's all right," Shane tells Joey. "There aren't any more guns in the valley." When Joey continues to protest his departure, Shane adds, "You go home to your mother and father and grow up to be strong and straight." To the degree that movies had a "message" for boys, it was that simple: If you do the right thing, you will grow up to be a man your parents will be proud of. Today, unfortunately, Hollywood encourages boys to be neither strong, nor straight.

CHAPTER 6

The Timely Man

It's a big joke that dads want to get the whole family to church an hour before services or to the airport three hours before a flight, but there's a reason behind it. Being organized and on time for everyday matters such as church or travel helps a man be ready when critical events demand prompt response. As my dad said: "Sleeping late makes your house stink." Wasting time is unmanly. He also said, "Time waits for no man." He didn't wait either. If you weren't ready for, say, a trip to the store for ice cream, he would leave without you.

Kids get their revenge on their parents when they become adolescents. A friend tells me he was never particularly conscious of time until his teenage daughters started dating. Then, in the lead-up to the agreed-upon curfew, the minutes slowed to hours and the anxiety ratcheted up with every passing minute. No matter the time of the curfew, my friend never fell asleep before his daughters came home. The sweetest sound on earth, he tells me, is the sound of the back door opening late at night; the later the arrival, the sweeter the sound. The sensation allows him to imagine how glorious the moment will be in heaven when a door opens and parents see a child who died before they did.

Time will always be part of our lives. The Western World took the lead in calculating time, and the United States in particular made time and timeliness national virtues. Until the fourteenth century, people relied largely on the sun and the moon to calculate time, but the invention of the mechanical clock put a little more order into a community's daily life. And communal the clocks were. Like the first public clock that appeared in Milan, Italy, in 1335, a single clock might keep a whole city—or monastery—apprised of the time.

A German, Heinrich De Vick, gets credit for the introduction in 1379 of a clock so functional and replicable it would serve as a model for most clocks for the next three centuries. The adaptation of the pendulum in the seventeenth century further improved the accuracy of clocks, and punctuality began to develop as a virtue, especially in the increasingly industrial parts of Northern Europe. It was in the late seventeenth century, in fact, that the word "punctual"—from the Latin *punctum*, "a point"—first entered the English language.

The first decade of the eighteenth century saw the birth of the multitalented man who all but Americanized time and its management, Benjamin Franklin. Born in Boston, the fifteenth of candlemaker Josiah Franklin's seventeen children, Franklin was sent to work as an indentured apprentice in his brother's print shop at age twelve. Industrious almost beyond belief, by twenty-two, Franklin was co-owner of a print shop. By twenty-six, he was publishing America's first German language newspaper. And at twenty-seven, he launched the highly successful annual publication *Poor Richard's Almanack*. It was from the *Almanack* and Franklin's 1758 *Autobiography*, also known as *The Way to Wealth*, that we get most of Franklin's famed quotes on the value of time.[1]

- Never leave that till tomorrow which you can do today.
- Dost thou love life? Then do not squander time, for that is the stuff life is made of.
- The way to wealth is as plain as the way to market. It depends chiefly on two words, industry and frugality: that is, waste neither time nor money, but make the best use of both. Without industry and frugality nothing will do, and with them everything.
- If time be of all things the most precious, wasting time must be the greatest prodigality.
- You may delay, but time will not, and lost time is never found again.
- He that riseth late must trot all day.
- Time is money.

In his autobiography, Franklin shares an hourly break-down of his average day. It begins at 5 a.m. with rising, washing, and contriving the day's business. He also allots time to pondering the morning question—"What good shall I do today?"—and, of course, to eating breakfast. From 8 a.m. to noon, Franklin works. From noon to 2 p.m., he dines, reviews his accounts, and reads. From 2 p.m. to 6 p.m., he works some more. Franklin devotes the hours from 6 p.m. to 10 p.m. to putting things away, supper, music, conversation, and an examination of the day in which he asks himself, "What good have I done today?" Franklin was more methodical than most men of his era—and more accomplished than any of them—but American ingenuity was prompting others to follow his example. They had to if they wanted to keep up with the pace of change.[2]

Increasingly, time was money. Railroad managers certainly thought so. When railroads first came on line in America in the 1820s and 1830s, managers realized they had a problem on their hands. Each community pegged its "noon" to the sun's peak in the sky. So while it might be 7:15 a.m. in New York, it could be 7:25 a.m. in Philadelphia and 7:40 a.m. in Pittsburgh. Before standardization, America had more than three hundred local time zones. In 1883, the railroads established four separate time zones and standardized times within those zones. It was not until 1918, however, that the U.S. government formally adopted railroad time as the national standard.[3]

The spread of time consciousness is captured in at least two classic westerns, 1957's *3:10 to Yuma*, remade in 2007, and of course, 1952's *High Noon*. Both capture the precision—and anxiety—that railroad time introduced into American life. Amplifying the anxiety was the telegraph, which was introduced at almost exactly the same time as the railroad. *High Noon* is set in 1898 in a town called Hadleyville in the New Mexico territory. The Hadleyville telegraph operator gets word that the notorious outlaw Frank Miller, sprung from prison, will be arriving on the noon train. As Marshal Will Kane (Gary Cooper) knows, Miller and his gang are coming to get revenge. Kane was the marshal who sent Miller to prison in the first place. Rather than flee, Kane knows that he must face Miller. As the town clocks tick away—they seem to be everywhere—Kane vainly pleads with the males in the town to help him.

Not only does the film capture the effect of time on the emerging American culture, but it also instructed a generation of men on the basics of manly honor. A man does not cut and run. Viewers instinctively despise those males who refuse Kane's request for help—all the while wondering if they would have done the same. Finally, it is Kane's new Quaker bride, Amy (Grace Kelly), who overcomes her religious scruples and shoots one of the men from behind, freeing Kane to kill Miller. When the townspeople celebrate Kane's triumph, he throws his marshal's badge in the dust and leaves town with Amy. The townsmen have been tested, and they failed. They were not ready for the moment, and Kane was not ready to forgive them. One reason my father reinforced the notion of time was to instill in us the need for readiness, the need to be prepared, the ability to rise to the occasion when time was of the essence.

In the twentieth century, time measurement became

more precise and time management became central to the way we lived. In 1910, a mechanical engineer named Frederick Winslow Taylor wrote *The Principles of Scientific Management*, one of the most influential management books of the century. Taylor helped popularize time and motion studies in business that gave rise to the age of the efficiency expert. Four years later saw America's first commercial flight. This industry launched a whole new level of time consciousness. To this day, among the most universal of nightmares is the "late for a flight" dream.

Not everyone welcomed our national focus on time management. Visitors from abroad still marvel at it, but it has undoubtedly helped transform America into the world's greatest industrial power. What made it work is that consciousness of time was bred into our DNA. We are a nation of self-starters. We set our own clocks. We don't wait for the factory whistle to blow or the cathedral bells to toll to tell us where to go or what to do.

The Academy Award–winning 2004 film *Crash* nicely captures this consciousness. In the penultimate scene of the film, Anthony, a street hood, drives a van he has stolen to a chop shop unaware of its contents. Lucien, the owner of the shop, opens the back of the van to find a dozen scared Asians padlocked together. Realizing these illegal immigrants have a street value as slave labor, Lucien offers to buy them from Anthony at $500 a head. Anthony finds his conscience and turns down the offer. Instead, he drives to Los Angeles's Chinatown, unlocks the shackled Asians, and sets them loose with the perfectly apt comment, "Come on—come on—come on, this is America, time is money."[4]

Time, of course, is more than just money. Time means responsibility: responsibility to God, responsibility to our fellow man, and responsibility to ourselves. More of a deist than a Christian, Franklin nonetheless hints at our debt to the divine when he says, "Dost thou love life? Then do not squander time, for that is the stuff life is made of."

The Bible's most elegant discourse on the subject of time can be found in Ecclesiastes 3. This is the verse that begins "To everything *there is* a season, A time for every purpose under heaven," and concludes, "A time to love, And a time to hate, A time of war, And a time of peace." So universal is its message that the Byrds, one of the hippest bands of the 1960s, recorded it with great respect for the lyrics and got a platinum record out of the deal. Although time was imprecisely measured two thousand years ago, the Old Testament and the New each speak to the necessity of using the time that God has given us as well as we can. As Paul told the Ephesians (5:15–16), "See then that you walk circumspectly, not as fools but as wise, redeeming the time, because the days are evil." To squander the time God has given us is to disrespect God.

Timeliness fuses naturally with chivalry. You don't need a great imagination to picture a young woman waiting anxiously to hear from the man she has recently met and to whom she has given her phone number. He knows she wants him to call, but he consciously delays. Why? Thoughtlessness? Gamesmanship? Callousness? Cowardice? No explanation speaks well of the male. Gents, this behavior may sound okay only until you picture your sister or your daughter waiting for that phone call.

In dealing with friends, family, and associates, a gentleman,

I believe, always respects their time. It is one thing to show up late at, say, a movie where no one is expecting you. It is another thing altogether to show up late for a meeting. If a dozen people are waiting for you, you have wasted as many minutes as you are late times twelve. If just a single person is waiting for you, the damage done is even greater. That person may worry about you, feel disrespected by you, or both. Not even an apology can compensate for the emotional damage you might have caused. In the words of William Shakespeare himself, "Better three hours too soon than a minute too late."[5]

Thanks to my father's training, I have always been ready for the moment. I have often been the youngest guy in the room. By the time I was twenty, I had served as student advocate for my school district, run (unsuccessfully) for a school board seat, served on the Dallas County Child Welfare Board and the Garland Parks and Recreation Board, and gotten a foothold in the media. Working in television has made me even more time conscious than I used to be. When I have a guest spot on a morning show, I set no fewer than three alarms to make sure I am primed and ready to go. If I don't, I will lose sleep worrying about whether I will wake up on time. To those who think our national concern with timeliness comes at the expense of "process," I would suggest they show up for a 7:15 a.m. guest spot at 7:30 a.m. and see how their career goes from there.

Like my father, I have trouble with the whole concept of "CPT," short for "colored people's time." The phrase suggests that it is a traditional part of Black culture to be habitually late for appointments, personal or professional. The phenomenon is not unique to Blacks. Almost everywhere in the world, when residents of a timeless rural culture intersect with a modern time-conscious culture, there will be miscommunication. Not surprisingly, the Great Migration from the South in the mid-twentieth century led to a major disconnect.

The problem comes when young people exploit the real lived experiences of their ancestors to claim for themselves an immunity to being on time. Especially in the age of COVID, I see among young adults of all races an indifference to punctuality. It is as if they were doing you a favor to show up at all. Youth is a terrible thing to squander. Martin Luther King Jr. was a twenty-six-year-old when he led the Montgomery bus boycott. Steve Jobs was twenty-one when he launched Apple. Stevie Wonder was thirteen and blind when he had his first number one hit single. God has a moment for all of us, and we have an obligation to be ready for it. To claim you don't know how to set an alarm clock is an insult to the God who created you.

"Timeliness is everything," Sean Hannity reminds me. He tells me of a billionaire friend for whom punctuality is among the highest of virtues. "If he tells me he is calling at five," says Hannity, "he will call at five. That old school philosophy worked for him his entire life." Without intending a pun, he adds, "The principles are timeless."

Finally, we have an obligation to ourselves to use our time wisely. "The proper function of man is to live, not to exist," said famed American author and outdoorsman Jack London. "I shall not waste my days in trying to prolong them. I shall use my time."[6] On reaching adulthood, who among us hasn't thought back to our younger days and regretted the time we wasted in endless time killers. Some, like watching sports on television or playing video games, are relatively benign. Others—like gambling, pornography, and drugs—are self-destructive.

Although the precise origin of the phrase is uncertain—it has been bouncing around in one form or another for two millennia—there is no denying its relevance: Idle hands are indeed the devil's workshop.

CHAPTER 7

The Resilient Man

The left doesn't want you to say "take it like a man" anymore, but there's a reason that phrase came about in the first place. Men are supposed to be able to deal with whatever comes their way without losing their cool or their ability to think clearly. That doesn't mean being superhuman, but it does mean having a mental playbook to turn to when faced with different kinds of challenges. Resilience simply means the ability to withstand adversity and bounce back from difficult life events.

Speaking of things superhuman, Chadwick Boseman earned international acclaim and my affection for his title role in the 2018 film *Black Panther*. The eighteenth film in the

Marvel Cinematic Universe (MCU), *Black Panther* was the first MCU film to center on a Black character and one of the increasingly rare MCU films to show a male in a heroic light.

Boseman knew something about resilience. He had been diagnosed with colon cancer two years before *Black Panther* debuted. Having created the character for an MCU film before his diagnosis and knowing the importance of the subsequent film for the Black community, Boseman kept working despite chemotherapy and several surgeries. Not wanting attention, he told only a trusted few of his struggles. His perseverance paid off. *Black Panther* was a hit with the critics and a huge commercial success. A professing Christian, Boseman honored his girlfriend's deepest wish and married her before he died in 2020 at just forty-three years of age.

No one understood the virtue of resilience—or explained it better—than President Theodore Roosevelt. In April 1910, Roosevelt delivered a speech titled "Citizenship in a Republic" at the Sorbonne, the venerable Parisian university. In the lengthy speech he took particular aim at those cynics and critics "who seek, in the affectation of contempt for the achievement of others, to hide from others and from themselves their own weakness." After reading what follows, I have to wonder what "T.R." would think of the psychologists who imaged traditional masculinity as "harmful":

> It is not the critic who counts; not the man who points out how the strong man stumbles, or where the doer of deeds could have done them better. The credit belongs to the man who is actually in the arena, whose face

is marred by dust and sweat and blood; who strives valiantly; who errs, who comes short again and again, because there is no effort without error and shortcoming; but who does actually strive to do the deeds; who knows the great enthusiasms, the great devotions; who spends himself in a worthy cause; who at the best knows in the end the triumph of high achievement, and who at the worst, if he fails, at least fails while daring greatly, so that his place shall never be with those cold and timid souls who neither know victory nor defeat.[1]

Roosevelt knew something about resilience. Sickly and asthmatic as a child, he could have surrendered to the comforts of his affluent New York City upbringing, but instead he confronted his own weakness through vigorous exercise and outdoor adventure. After the death of his wife and mother on the same day in 1880, Roosevelt found emotional refuge in the western wilderness. There he learned to ride western style, rope, and hunt. He developed a respect for the men he met along the way. The cowboy possessed, said Roosevelt, "few of the emasculated, milk-and-water moralities admired by the pseudo-philanthropists; but he does possess, to a very high degree, the stern, manly qualities that are invaluable to a nation."[2]

When war with Spain broke out in 1898, Roosevelt quit his desk job in Washington as assistant secretary of the Navy and formed, against the advice of friends and family, his own cavalry unit. The volunteer unit included cowboys, Indians, and upscale gentlemen looking for adventure. On July 1, 1998, they found plenty of it when Roosevelt led the "Rough Riders'" famously successful charge up San Juan Hill.

Today, in the absence of war, the sports world offers us perhaps the clearest and best-known examples of how a resilient man behaves when faced with obstacles. Muhammad Ali sacrificed his heavyweight championship title to protest the War in Vietnam. Forced to remain idle during four prime years of his career, Ali returns to the ring in 1971, only to be hammered by Joe Frazier in what many experts consider the "fight of the century."

Undaunted, Ali endures a series of bruising fights for three years to earn a title shot and prevails over champion George Foreman in the famed "Rumble in the Jungle." Says Ali, "Only a man who knows what it is like to be defeated can reach down to the bottom of his soul and come up with the extra ounce of power it takes to win when the match is even."[3]

Rocky Bleier takes another path. After being captain of the Notre Dame football team, Bleier is drafted in the sixteenth round by the Pittsburgh Steelers. He barely makes the team as a running back and gets just nine touches his rookie season. In 1969, the U.S. Army drafts him, and Bleier volunteers for Vietnam. In August 1969, Private Bleier is shot in the leg. Minutes later, a grenade explodes next to him. Doctors extract more than one hundred pieces of shrapnel and encourage him by saying he may one day walk again.

Bleier has more ambitious goals. The Steelers stick by him. They put him on injured reserve in 1970, and in 1971, he plays on special teams. On two occasions, the Steelers waive him, but Bleier never gives up. He trains ferociously to regain his old form, and by 1974, he is a starter. That year, the Steelers go on to win the Super Bowl and repeat with Bleier playing a key role in 1975, 1978, and 1979. Says Bleier, "The lessons I learned in Vietnam and in the NFL reinforced one another: teamwork, sacrifice, responsibility, accountability, and leadership."[4]

If there is a poster child for resilience in the world of sports, it would have to be Jim Valvano, a point guard at Rutgers, an NCAA Championship–winning coach at North Carolina State, and a successful broadcaster thereafter. In June 1992, having just been cleared of the NCAA violations that cost him his coaching job, Valvano was diagnosed with metastatic adenocarcinoma.

Nine months later, Valvano was presented with the inaugural Arthur Ashe Courage and Humanitarian Award at the ESPY Award Show. It was here that Valvano showed what resilience was all about. Barely able to walk to the stage, he gave the most compelling speech in sports history since Lou Gehrig's Yankee farewell in 1939. Colorful to the end, Valvano talked about his role in starting the Jimmy V Cancer Foundation. "Its motto," he told the crowd, "is 'Don't give up. Don't ever give up.' And that's what I'm going to try to do every minute that I have left. I will thank God for the day and the moment I have.

"I know I've got to go. I've got to go, and I got one last thing," Valvano declared. "I've said it before and I'm gonna say it again. Cancer can take away all my physical abilities. It cannot touch my mind. It cannot touch my heart. And it cannot touch my soul. And those three things are going to carry on forever. I thank you and God bless y'all."[5] Valvano died eight weeks later at age forty-seven. In the thirty years since, the V Foundation has funded more than three hundred million dollars' worth of cancer research nationwide.

Although the resilient man is not necessarily a Godly man, in my experience those who walk in the way of the Lord will walk farther and longer than those who don't. I continue to be impressed by the number of athletes, especially quarterbacks, who openly profess their faith in Jesus. That faith does not guarantee victory, but it can surely make a man more resilient in the face of adversity.

Career backup quarterback Nick Foles made this case after stepping in for the injured Carson Wentz to lead the Philadelphia Eagles to a Super Bowl win over Tom Brady and the Patriots in 2018. "Failure is a part of life. That's a part of building character and growing. Like, without failure, who would you be? I wouldn't be up here if I hadn't fallen thousands of times, made mistakes," said the proudly Christian Foles in his post-game interview. "I might be in the NFL, and we might have just won the Super Bowl, but hey, we still have daily struggles. I still have daily struggles. But that's where my faith comes in. That's where my family comes in."[6]

In generations past, young males were routinely exposed to stories like these either through the media or through books or through school. A heroic figure faces obstacles and persists despite setbacks and injuries and rejection. Today, in the age of identity politics, such stories all too often focus on the obstacle to be overcome. In so doing, they ignore the resilience of the hero and dwell on the presumed endurance of the obstacle.

In 1997, for instance, then President Bill Clinton presided over a celebration marking the fiftieth anniversary of Jackie Robinson's breakthrough appearance as a Major League baseball player. If anyone personified resilience, it was Robinson. Born in Georgia, he had the good fortune of moving to Southern California as a boy. There he attended integrated public schools all the way through college at UCLA. At every stop, he proved to be an extraordinary athlete and a model student. In 1942, Robinson was drafted into the U.S. Army, then at war, applied for Officer's Training School, and was honorably discharged in late 1944 as a captain.

The war helped America grow up. Sensing change in the air, Brooklyn Dodgers president Branch Rickey scouted the Negro baseball leagues, not necessarily for the best player, but for the most resilient very good player. Although Robinson never rolled over for anyone, even in the Army, he knew he had to rise above the inevitable abuse that would come his way as the first Black player in the major leagues.

And abuse he got. It would have been more abuse than someone less proud and less confident could endure, but endure Robinson did, in the process winning millions of hearts and minds, not to mention the Dodgers' first World Series. "Jackie was out front all the time," former teammate Ralph Branca told the *Washington Post*. "That first year—razzed, heckled, adverse conditions, playing a new position. He answered back with his bat, with his feet, with his brain." Added Branca, "Jackie made it easy for Martin Luther King."[7] Appropriately enough, Chadwick Boseman played Robinson in the popular 2013 film *42*.

In 1997, the Clinton White House and its allies used the occasion of Robinson's anniversary less to celebrate Robinson than to exploit his memory. Central to this exploitation was the insistence that little had changed in the fifty years since Robinson's debut. As the *Post* noted, "On a cold night at Shea Stadium, President Clinton warned against any conclusion that Robinson's job is complete." The *Post* quoted Clinton as saying, "We can do better. We need to establish equality in the boardrooms of baseball and corporate America."

What Robinson fought for was "equality" of opportunity. Sports may well be America's last meritocracy. There is no equality once a player takes the field. Some players are measurably better than others. Robinson was one of the best. He was named National League MVP in 1949 not to satisfy a quota but because he hit .342, drove in 124 runs, and stole 37 bases. By comparing Robinson's breakthrough to a perceived lack of equity in the front offices only served to diminish Robinson's accomplishment.

Caught in the backwash between equity and equality was the then twenty-one-year-old golf phenom Tiger Woods, who, days earlier, had just won his first major championship, the Masters. When he turned down Clinton's invitation to appear at the Robinson celebration, he rendered himself suspect in the eyes of those whose livelihood was based on feeding grievances.

Woods, however, did not think himself worthy of the comparison to Robinson. As he himself has acknowledged, he has never suffered more from being a person of color than the occasional raised eyebrow. On top of that, upon turning pro, he was flooded with the most lucrative endorsement deals in golf history. Fifty years after Robinson's debut, Woods's ethnic background made him more attractive to advertisers, not less.

The real pioneers, Woods was the first to admit, were professional Black golfers a generation ahead of him like Lee Elder and Charlie Sifford. "What people don't realize is the amount of harassment that he had to go through just to play," said Woods on the occasion of Elder's death in 2021. "The fierceness to fight for something you believe in. I don't think he gets enough credit."[8] Woods has also run afoul of the grievance industry by embracing his mixed race heritage, famously calling himself on one occasion "'Cablinasian'—a mix of Caucasian, black, (American) Indian and Asian."[9] He refused to write his mother, who was born in Thailand, out of his racial identity, and critics have never forgiven him for doing that.

All that said, no athlete has faced more adversity or proved more resilient than Tiger Woods. A few of his wounds have been self-inflicted, but they have been no less real because of his own misjudgments. In the memorable 2008 U.S. Open, for instance, Woods grimaced his way through the tournament playing with two stress fractures in his tibia and a knee that would require surgery a week afterward. Woods had to sink a fifteen-foot birdie putt on the eighteenth hole of the final round just to tie, and that he did. A tie meant an eighteen-hole showdown with Rocco Mediate the next day. When that, too, ended in a tie, the limping Woods found the will to play one more sudden death hole, and there he sealed his victory.

After the 2019 Masters Tournament, Woods received nearly as much attention in the health journals as he did in the sports media. Just to tee off, Woods had to endure four back surgeries in the previous five years. These were in addition to his four previous knee surgeries and a chronic Achilles tendon ailment. If that were not challenge enough, Woods was now forty-three years old. As Woods observed upon winning, "I had serious doubts after what transpired a couple years ago. I could barely walk. I couldn't sit. Couldn't lay down. I really couldn't do much of anything."[10] Woods persisted through it all. That's just who he is and how he was raised by his father, Earl Woods. "Well, you never give up," added Tiger. "That's a given. You always fight. Just giving up's never in the equation."[11]

As useful as athletes are as role models for young males, they have little effect on the well-being of the average citizen. Inventors, however, are another story. Consider, for instance, the world of 1890. At the time, the average American family was living in a home without electricity, running water, indoor plumbing, central heating, or a telephone. They had never ridden in a car, had never seen a movie or listened to a phonograph, and had no concept of an airplane. By 1920, however, the average middle-class person in urban America had electricity, running water, indoor plumbing, central heating, a telephone, a phonograph, and a car in the driveway. Some would have even flown on airplanes, and just about all would have seen a movie.

The men responsible for this transformation had at least one character trait in common—yes, resilience. They also had the good fortune of living in the one country that encouraged and rewarded individual initiative more than any other. That same country, however, did not provide these men a safety net. If they failed, they failed. There were no bailouts or government grants. We know today only those men who persisted despite their failures. There were many who did not succeed.

The men most prominent in this revolution—Thomas Edison, Henry Ford, the Wright brothers—all were born into humble families in the Midwest in the mid-nineteenth century. None of them graduated from high school. All were inventive and entrepreneurial from a young age, and all failed more often than they succeeded.

At this point, I imagine equity proponents griping that these are all white men, presumably straight at that. What they fail to understand is that for all the roadblocks Blacks faced in the nineteenth century, the entrepreneurial route was largely left open. The famously inventive agronomist George Washington Carver, for instance, was born in the Midwest a year after Henry Ford into even humbler surroundings, his parents being slaves. He, too, was a tinkerer and a self-starter. Unlike the others, however, Carver graduated from college.

I take a greater interest in the Wright brothers for a few reasons. One is that I spend so much time in the air. Frequent flier that I am, I still marvel at the improbability of working comfortably on my laptop five miles above the surface of the earth. Although I do not fear flying, I think it perfectly understandable that some people do. And that brings us to the second reason the Wright brothers interest me. Although all invention involves some danger—I suspect Edison got more than a few shocks in his life—the Wright brothers faced injury, even death, with every failed experiment. Yet they persisted.

Pulitzer Prize winner David McCullough knew something about persistence too. He was eighty-two when he wrote his award-winning book *The Wright Brothers*. Forty-seven years earlier, McCullough wrote his first book, *The Johnstown Flood*, while working around a full-time government job. I suspect he could identify with Wilbur and Orville Wright. Not unlike Benjamin Franklin, Orville launched his own printing business while still a teenager. Wilbur helped him and soon thereafter the brothers launched a weekly newspaper in Dayton, Ohio, where they were living. Encouraged by its success, the Wrights launched a daily newspaper but that failed, and they switched to commercial printing. Among their clients was a Black friend of Orville's, Paul Laurence Dunbar, who would later achieve international fame as a poet and writer.

In the 1890s, the bicycle craze struck America, and the brothers switched gears to capitalize on it. They began with a repair shop, and by 1896, they were manufacturing their own bicycles. They invested the money they made to fund their experiments in heavier-than-air flight. The fact that they were competing against the Smithsonian Institution to be first in the air as well as government-funded operations in Europe did not discourage them.

Failure haunted the brothers at every turn, but they soldiered on. McCullough documents their many setbacks as well as their impressive resilience in the face of seeming defeat. Some excerpts relating to this resilience:

Along with the costs of experiments in flight, the risks of humiliating failure, injury, and, of course, death, there was the inevitable prospect of being mocked as a crank, a crackpot, and in many cases with good reason.[12]

...because of his failure to find the spruce spars needed...[13]

A failure of a motor will then mean simply a slow descent and safe landing instead of a disastrous fall.[14]

Finally, after several more failed attempts, he moved back nearly a foot from where he started and sailed off more than 100 yards.[15]

...which consumed far more time and attention than the brothers wished and proved a total failure.[16]

After Herring failed several times to get the cumbersome three-wing machine off the ground, Wilbur and Orville each gave it a try and did no better.[17]

But when the next day they started up the motor, the magneto...failed to deliver a spark to ignite the gas and the vibrations of the misfiring engine tore loose and badly twisted the propeller shafts.[18]

It would be speculated later by some that the failure that day had been a hoax staged as a way to deflate further interest by the public and the press. [It wasn't.][19]

...a first public demonstration that failed in almost any way would be a serious setback.[20]

This was so great a failure that it was some years before another crossed my field of vision.[21]

Unlike several of their competitors, the Wright brothers survived their miscalculations. Resilient almost to a fault, they persisted, and on December 17, 1903, both brothers succeeded in getting the plane off the ground. Orville's description of the day's longest flight speaks to the risks inherent even in success:

Wilbur started the fourth and last flight at just about 12 o'clock. The first few hundred feet were up and down, as before, but by the time three hundred ft had been covered, the machine was under much better control. The course for the next four or five hundred feet had but little undulation. However, when out about eight hundred feet the machine began pitching again, and, in one of its darts downward, struck the ground. The distance over the ground was measured to be 852 feet; the time of the flight was 59 seconds. The frame supporting the front rudder was badly broken, but the main part of the machine was not injured at all. We estimated that the machine could be put in condition for flight again in about a day or two.[22]

The *New York Times* thought it "a highly significant fact that, until the Wrights succeeded, all attempts at flight with heavier-than-air machines were dismal failures but since they showed the thing could be done everybody seems able to do it."[23] That's what pioneers do. They clear the way for others.

Skeptics about the American experiment like to think that the opportunities for people as ordinary as a bicycle repairman to succeed on a grand scale are a thing of centuries past. I imagine them typing out such thoughts on their MacBook Air in between calls on their iPhones without ever reflecting where their MacBooks and iPhones come from. The man behind both those devices had roots as humble as those of Edison or the Wright brothers.

Born in 1955 to a Syrian father and a German-American mother, Steve Jobs was given up for adoption at birth. Jobs's biological mother at first insisted that the adoptive parents be college educated—Paul and Clara Jobs were not—but relented when the couple promised to send the boy to college. It was a wiser decision than the mom knew. Paul Jobs was a nineteenth-century kind of guy, a machinist, a mechanic, "an inveterate tinkerer" in the Wright brothers tradition. Write Jobs biographers Brent Schlender and Rick Tetzeli, Paul "taught his son the paramount value of taking one's time, paying attention to details, and—since Paul was anything but rich—putting in the legwork to hunt for spare parts that were a good value."[24]

There is no overestimating the value for a boy of having a father in the home. When Steve was about five or six, Paul sectioned off a part of his workbench and said to his son, "Steve, this is your workbench now."[25] It is highly unlikely that Steve would have grown up to become "Steve Jobs" in any other kind of household. Steve knew it. Although not known for his kindness, Jobs always had a soft spot for his father. "He spent a lot of time with me," said Jobs, "teaching me how to build things, take things apart, put things back together."[26] Following in his father's footsteps, Steve, too, became a tinkerer. Growing up as he did in Silicon Valley, it was almost inevitable that his tinkering would turn to electronics.

Good as their word, Paul and Clara sent Steve off to college, but they couldn't keep him there. After a semester Jobs dropped out, not wanting to waste his parents' money on an education that was irrelevant to him. Tired of dabbling in the many cults and vices available to a young California male, Jobs returned to Silicon Valley, hooked up with friend Steve Wozniak, and launched Apple Computers from the family garage in 1976 when Jobs was just twenty-one. The family home is now a national historic site.

Like the Wright brothers, Jobs would have his ups and downs. If the downs weren't as life threatening as they were for Wilbur and Orville, they were more public, more humiliating. Tracking the word "fail" through Schlender and Tetzeli's book gives some sense of the trials Jobs would endure before finally breaking through later in his life.

But Steve was a failure at managing this group.[27]

Twice now in rapid succession, Steve had failed...[28]

An alarming number of Apple III's started suffering catastrophic failures due to overheating.[29]

The Apple III was an unmitigated commercial failure.[30]

Steve's own failures did nothing to chasten him.[31]

His career to this point consisted of a couple of failures—his work on Apple III and the LISA—and a couple of breakthrough products.[32]

It's just that in decision after decision, Steve failed to account for the trade-offs that accompanied his fanciful choices.[33]

It shouldn't be surprising, then, that Steve failed to make this important relationship work.[34]

He killed the IBM deal by failing to follow through as a good business partner.[35]

NeXT failed at all of that.[36]

There was no hiding the fact that NeXT's failure was primarily Steve's doing.[37]

The Steve Jobs story was starting to shift from his past successes to his present failures.[38]

In 1986, after having been bounced from Apple, the company he cofounded, Jobs paid $10 million to buy a struggling animation group soon to be known as Pixar. Jobs continued to pour more of his Apple buyout millions into Pixar until it finally hit pay dirt with the release of the blockbuster animated film *Toy Story*. "[Pixar] should have failed," cofounder Alvy Ray Smith told one interviewer, "but it seemed to me that Steve just would not suffer another defeat."[39]

In 1996, Jobs returned to Apple, and success followed success. The iPod followed the iMac, and iPad followed the iPhone. Apple was breaking new ground and making great profits. In 2003, with the turnaround well underway, the forty-eight-year-old Jobs was diagnosed with cancer. In August 2011, he announced his retirement as Apple CEO. Six weeks later, he was dead.

Jobs had come a long way. "The failures, stinging reversals, miscommunications, bad judgment calls, emphases on wrong values—the whole Pandora's box of immaturity," write Schlender and Tetzeli, "were necessary prerequisites to the clarity, moderation, reflection, and steadiness he would display in later years."[40] Jobs remained an imperfect man, but a man he was, and there was no doubting his resilience.

In 2013, when I was just twenty and a student at the University of North Texas, I had the good fortune of working with James O'Keefe, the founder of Project Veritas and one of the most creative and resilient men in American media.

When I met O'Keefe, he had not yet turned thirty himself, but he had already accomplished more—and suffered more setbacks—than anyone in journalism, no matter what their age. In 2009, O'Keefe and his twenty-three-year-old partner, Hannah Giles, working off James's credit cards, posed as a pimp and a prostitute in order to expose the underbelly of the alleged anti-poverty group ACORN. O'Keefe and Giles visited several ACORN offices across the country, covertly recording ACORN workers as they advised the pair on how best to run a business that employed underage sex workers smuggled into the country. With the help of Andrew Breitbart, they aired the videos one after another and shocked the nation. As a result of their work, the Census Bureau and the Department of Housing and Urban Development severed their relations with ACORN. Better still, the GOP introduced a "Defund ACORN Act" in a Democratic House, and it passed overwhelmingly.

A self-starter, O'Keefe was improvising his journalistic model as he moved from investigation to investigation. Not all projects worked, especially after the successful ACORN sting put a bull's-eye on O'Keefe's back. In January 2010, in New Orleans for a separate investigation, O'Keefe and a few friends decided to test the claim of Senator Mary Landrieu of Louisiana that Tea Party members could not get through to her office because of the excess volume of calls. With two of the group of four guys posing as telephone repairmen, they visited Landrieu's New Orleans office.

This hastily thought-out plan backfired. The FBI arrested the four under the trumped-up charge of entering a federal building under "false pretenses" although all of them used their real IDs. In an early preview of how a politicized Department of Justice works, the four were hustled off to jail, where they remained until processed a day later. The media were delighted to misreport their "crime." MSNBC took to calling it "Watergate Jr." despite the fact that these guys had no tools and no intent of bugging anything.[41]

A hero on the right just months earlier, O'Keefe was now a pariah in a political party known for its spinelessness. Another public failure brought him even more grief. His lowest moment found him, as he writes in his book *Breakthrough*, "living at home, stuck in Jersey, mired in debt, abandoned by my allies, estranged from my friends, unable to sleep, unwilling to eat, my career in tatters, crushed by the weight of it all, and praying not for a miracle, but just some relief."[42]

O'Keefe contemplated his future from a pew at St. Gabriel the Archangel Church in Saddle River, New Jersey. He had in his possession a series of undercover tapes he recorded that revealed the corruption at the heart of the New Jersey Education Association, a teachers' union. He did not know whether he had the strength to put himself out in public one more time, knowing that even people on his own side wanted him to just go away.

"I asked myself whether I could justify taking the risks anymore, whether I could endure the lies of my enemies and the defamation of the machine," O'Keefe writes. "But I knew then that as long as I had my family and my faith in God, I was going to be okay. I immediately felt renewed. It was out of my hands now."[43] Not all resilient men turn to God, but those who do find a strength they were not sure they had.

O'Keefe did. By the time I met up with him three years after his near surrender, he had managed to refine his techniques and become his own brand.

When I was recommended to O'Keefe, I was just twenty years old and a recovering Democrat. Having been a party activist, I knew how the Democrats worked. They monopolized the staffs of allegedly nonpartisan organizations and all too often used the data gleaned and the contacts made for partisan ends. At the time, Obamacare was just coming online. What the Obama administration did was to use nonprofit groups to provide "navigators" to help people access this complex and confusing program. In historic Democratic fashion, they would actually contract with partisan groups hiding their real agenda. The navigators, in turn, would use the data they secured to update Democratic prospect lists.

So I went undercover for O'Keefe. This involved training in the legal and ethical considerations of undercover work as well as in the technical challenges of wearing a hidden camera. Although I had many potential targets on my list, the fellow I set my sights on was Chris Tarango, then the Texas communications director for Enroll America, an NGO dedicated to signing people up for Obamacare. Having wrangled a meeting, I was given a cover story, namely that I had a wealthy uncle who was interested in purchasing a database of Obamacare enrollees for use by his political action committee. I was wearing a hidden camera. As I quickly came to understand, this was nerve-wracking work. When Tarango asked me my uncle's name, a question I was not expecting, I panicked and blurted out, "Danny Glover."

"The actor?" he asked.

"Same name," I stuttered, feeling totally foolish and exposed.

Tarango should have rejected my request out of hand, but he didn't. Instead, he said on camera, "I talk to one person that I think might be open to having this conversation behind closed doors."

Bill O'Reilly aired the exchange, as did local TV news stations. Enroll America promptly put out a statement assuring citizens that its employees "absolutely don't work with any partisan organizations, campaigns, or candidates." Enroll America went on to say that "even the suggestion by any of our staff that such activity could occur is inappropriate, and the employee seen in the video has resigned from his role in Enroll America."[44]

Tarango was toast. So, in a sense, was I. Although I was not seen on camera, I was heard. People quickly figured out that I was the undercover guy, and some proceeded to make my life very difficult. Losing "friends" was to be expected. Having my apartment broken into and searched by persons unknown was not. I got a sense of what it felt like to be a pariah, much as O'Keefe must have experienced in his early days and maybe even today. As I write this, O'Keefe has just been forced out of Project Veritas by his board for reasons only God can discern.

Although I had done what a journalist should do, namely expose corruption, some in the Black community turned against me. They were not interested in honest government. They were interested, it seemed, in winning elections. I had been leading marches since grade school, but skeptics now doubted my commitment to the community. Rather than cut and run, I redoubled my efforts and reinforced my community roots. Half the things I did no one knows, but the investments I made and the relationships I established were substantial and enduring. As Jesus reminds us in Luke 4:24, "Assuredly, I say to you, no prophet is accepted in his own country." Rejection is part of life, always has been. A man, I have learned, persists in spite of it.

When conservatives in the public arena fail, they face an additional challenge. As O'Keefe has experienced any number of times, especially with his departure from Project Veritas, the media revel in any hint of failure. Resilient as always, O'Keefe responded to his ouster with the creation of the instantly successful O'Keefe Media Group. OMG, indeed!

If a conservative's failure involves a departure from Biblical values, the media do a veritable end zone dance. I talked to Pete Hegseth about this double standard. Having been the subject of headlines such as, WORDS AND DEEDS OUT OF ALIGNMENT FOR POTENTIAL CABINET APPOINTMENT AND FOX NEWS PERSONALITY, he was in a position to know.[45] This is the kind of headline Hunter Biden and other leftists never have to face. Professing no recognizable moral values, they are all but immune to the charge of hypocrisy.

No need for detail here, but Hegseth will be the first to admit he has made mistakes. From Adam's time to today, we all have. The resilient man seeks forgiveness for the brokenness he has caused and realigns his values with those of the Bible, the best of all possible guides. "A big part of manhood is admitting you're wrong and learning something new and adjusting your course," he tells me. As a father, Hegseth feels a particular responsibility to model behavior he would want his young sons to emulate. Virtues like faith, discipline, respect, studiousness, and hard work do not come naturally. It is a father's duty to introduce them and to apply them as a parent. "If [males] are tethered to Biblical wisdom," says Hegseth, "they will be tethered to the truth."

CHAPTER 8

The Fit Man

"I welcome this opportunity to speak to the people of America about a subject which I believe to be most important," said newly inaugurated President John F. Kennedy in 1961, "and that is the subject of physical fitness." Kennedy promptly used his bully pulpit to put his sentiments into action.

Although the president lacked the authority to mandate a renewed interest in physical fitness, he did the next best thing. He launched a White House Committee on Health and Fitness that cajoled thousands of schools across the country to adopt a recommended curriculum and to challenge their students to meet the requisite goals. The program actually worked, at least for a while.

I learned of President Kennedy's commitment to physical fitness watching a Fox Nation special by my then colleague Tucker Carlson with the chilling title "The End of Men."[1] The special documented the tangible decline in fitness among young men since the 1960s as well as the very real, and possibly related, decline in sperm count. "Spermageddon," some are calling it. Although there is little as individuals we can do to address these societal declines, we have full control about our personal destiny.

"Mental and physical vigor go hand in hand," said President Kennedy, and I have come to agree. As an athlete coming of age, I took my fitness for granted. I was always trim and presumed I always would be. Then I moved to Washington, an unhealthy city on any number of levels. In DC, virtually all relationships are transactional. There, people have less interest in who you are than what you do.

My job was to run *Campus Reform*. As a Black American leading a conservative-leaning organization, I fit uneasily into DC culture. I compensated by working long hours and attending all the formal lunches and dinners to which I was invited. The weight gain kind of snuck up on me. I looked in the mirror one day and said out loud, "Damn, you look fat."

Some other people noticed as well. One was my Texas friend Jack Brewer, a former NFL safety. Jack ribbed me mercilessly, and I deserved it. When I interviewed him for this book, he shared with me his philosophy of fitness. "When you are fit, you are more aware, you care more," he explains. He contends that if you let yourself go physically, you will be more inclined to let yourself go spiritually as well. "You've got to keep yourself together," he adds.

He has a point. I had gained an unbelievable seventy-five pounds. There I drew the line. I refused to buy clothes to fit my new bulk and resolved instead to move comfortably back into the clothes I already had. I began by adopting the diet plan of actor (not NBA great) Michael B. Jordan, which includes lots of nutritious grains, green veggies, and lean protein. This is the diet Jordan used to ready himself for his role as Creed in the *Rocky* sequels.

I supplemented the diet with a 5 a.m. workout and another workout at the end of the day. In ten weeks, I lost fifty pounds and gained a ton of energy. If we are to do the work that God put us here to do, we do it much better—and potentially live longer—when we stay fit. Married men owe this much to their wives and children. Single men owe it to their employers and themselves.

Of all the professional athletes, perhaps none understood the responsibility to stay fit better than the Los Angeles Lakers' superstar Kobe Bryant. Not everyone who played with Bryant liked him, but they all respected his commitment to the fans, to the ownership, and to his own legacy. In 2009, reporter Rick Reilly, then with ESPN, documented an entire day with Bryant, who, he writes, "has been known to get up earlier than many barn owls to conduct his famously brutal workouts." In describing the workout, Reilly warns his readers, "If you don't want to feel like a complete jelly-filled donut, don't read this next part."[2]

The then thirty-year-old Bryant, in the thirteenth season of a twenty-year career, was intent on carrying the Lakers to the NBA championships. He felt he owed it to his teammates to stay as fit as possible. He owed it to his family to get up and out early so he could spend as much time as possible with his daughters. As Bryant knew better than anyone, a 2003 incident in a Colorado hotel almost cost him both family and team. "But my wife and I, we toughed it out," he told Reilly. "She and I, we got through it. We're going to be celebrating our eight-year anniversary together. And when I think about how I almost lost it, the family and everything, I'm just very thankful, and blessed. It was really close there for a while."

Bryant and the Lakers went on to win the 2009 NBA championship with Bryant being named MVP. A family man to the end, in January 2020, Bryant was taking his thirteen-year-old daughter, Gianna, two of her teammates, and her teammates' parents to a basketball game when their chartered helicopter crashed, killing everyone on board. As it happens, Bryant died just before the COVID-19 pandemic struck, and the nation slipped into a physical and emotional malaise from which it has yet to recover.

What I am saying, I know, cuts across the grain. Today, the very word "fat" has become taboo. Obese entertainers are now celebrated and overweight models grace the covers of our magazines. In 2022, *Sports Illustrated*, celebrating an "inclusive range of backgrounds and body types," put a conspicuously heavyset woman on the cover of its famed annual swimsuit edition. A Gatorade TV ad features a woman at least one hundred pounds overweight exercising in a clingy two-piece outfit. For the record, a twelve-ounce bottle of Gatorade has eighty more calories than a twelve-ounce bottle of water.

The timing for this trend could not be worse. In addition to being a risk factor in heart disease and cancer, obesity emerged as a lethal variable during the COVID-19 era. As the CDC quietly admitted, "Having obesity may triple the risk of hospitalization due to a COVID-19 infection."[3] It was the one risk factor that the individual could control, but the one that media, even health experts, feared to mention lest the culture shame them.

People died out of ignorance. Authorities closed gyms and parks and locked in their citizens. As a result, three times as many people gained weight as lost it during the pandemic, with the obese reporting the most weight gain.[4] The policies designed to protect people left them even more vulnerable to the disease they were hiding from.

Of late, Hollywood has made its peace with obesity, but this has not always been the case. In fact, there have been many great movies made about sports and fitness, the *Rocky/Creed* series prominent among them. The original *Rocky* won the Academy Award for best picture in 1977, but since then only one sports movie has won top honors, the surprise hit *Chariots of Fire* in 1982.

What made the award even more surprising is that *Chariots of Fire* deals in a positive way with the protagonist's Christianity. The movie tells the largely true story of Eric Liddell, a Scottish missionary in training whose running ambitions sometimes conflict with and sometimes reinforce his faith. The movie tells the parallel story of Harold Abrahams, a Jewish student athlete and fellow Cambridge student, who runs in no small part to subvert British class and race prejudices.

Admittedly, Liddell was not American, but the movie resonates with so many of us in part because the Scottish and Scotch-Irish brand of evangelical Christianity deeply influenced the development of the Church in America, including the Black Church. Great Britain was, after all, our mothership. Abrahams was not American either, but American Jews and other disfavored ethnics can identify with his struggles. Then, too, once a movie wins an Oscar, it becomes part of American culture, regardless of its source.

Liddell faces resistance both from within his own family and from larger British society. His sister, Jenny, challenges Liddell on his motives for running, questioning whether it is a distraction from his larger mission. Reflecting on her criticism, Liddell sees a higher purpose for his track career. "I have no formula for winning the race," he says at one point. "Everyone runs in her own way, or his own way. And where does the power come from, to see the race to its end? From within." Liddell then quotes Jesus from Luke 17:21, "Behold, the Kingdom of God is within you." Liddell explains, "If you commit yourself to the love of Christ, then that is how you run a straight race."

Liddell sees his gift as a way to glorify God. "God made me fast. And when I run, I feel His pleasure," he observes. My friend Jack Brewer feels much the same about his physical gifts. "I saw so many people waste God's gifts because they were unfit. I have at least six cousins who were better than me," says the NFL veteran. "It was heartbreaking."

Liddell was not about to squander his gifts. Accordingly, he feels the obligation not only to purify his own soul but also to give public witness to his faith. This requires total commitment but only if that commitment does not conflict with his faith. As he discovers, it will. The 1924 Olympics committee schedules the 100-meter heats for a Sunday. Several powerful British leaders lean on Liddell to compromise his faith.

He refuses. "God made countries. God makes kings, and the rules by which they govern," Liddell tells them. "And those rules say that the Sabbath is his. And I for one intend to keep it that way." Liddell stands by his principles, and Abrahams wins the 100-meter. Liddell switches to the 400-meter, scheduled for a Thursday, and wins that. Unusual for a sports film, the movie's Hollywood ending reflects what happened in real life. Liddell stood by his commitment. The following year, he went to China to continue his missionary work and eventually died there in a Japanese concentration camp.

Another world-class athlete who found himself in a Japanese concentration camp was Louis Zamperini, the protagonist of Laura Hillenbrand's 2010 mega bestseller *Unbroken: A World War II Story of Survival, Resilience, and Redemption*, and the 2014 film of the same name. The son of Italian immigrants, Louis was raised in a devoutly Catholic home in California. When he started school, Louis could barely speak English. This led to the inevitable bullying. To preserve his dignity, Louis fought back and got into more trouble than was good for him. An older brother turned him on to track as a way to discipline his energy, and there Louis found his passion.

Louis proved to be something of a prodigy as a long-distance runner. As a nineteen-year-old, he made the U.S. Olympic team. He saw this as the first step in his goal to being the world's best in the 5,000-meter race. In the infamous 1936 Olympics, Louis was already good enough to come in eighth. Although World War II put the Olympics on hold for twelve years and killed Louis's Olympic dreams, the discipline he learned as an athlete would soon pay off in ways the young Olympian could never have anticipated.

His story is incredible. I do it an injustice by abridging it, but his life speaks so well to the theme of this chapter, "The Fit Man," it begs inclusion. A patriot, Louis enlisted in the U.S. Army Air Forces before Pearl Harbor. He quickly earned a commission as a second lieutenant and served as a bombardier on a B-24 Liberator named "Super Man." The plane earned its nickname.

In April 1943, Super Man survived a hundred or so rounds from three Japanese Zeros and limped back into base with five of its crew wounded, one mortally. Miraculously unscathed, Louis tended to the wounded on the flight back and was credited with saving the lives of two of them.

In between missions, Louis continued to train. In May 1943, he ran a mile in four minutes and twelve seconds. At the time, no one had yet run a mile in under four minutes. Louis might have been the first, but fate intervened once again. Later that same month, while on a search and rescue mission nearly a thousand miles south of Hawaii, Louis's plane crashed, killing eight of the eleven men on board instantly. Louis survived the crash along with two others, Russell Phillips and Francis McNamara. After thirty-three harrowing days at sea, McNamara died. "Though all three men faced the same hardship, their differing perceptions of it appeared to be shaping their fates," writes Hillenbrand. "Louis and Phil's hope displaced their fear and inspired them to work toward their survival, and each success renewed their physical and emotional vigor. Mac's resignation seemed to paralyze him and the less he participated in their efforts to survive, the more he slipped."[5]

Louis and Phil would spend a record forty-seven days at sea before washing ashore in the Marshall Islands. Unfortunately, the Japanese controlled the islands and promptly took the two starving men prisoners. What Louis experienced on the raft was a leisure cruise compared to what would happen in the next two years. Knowing he was an Olympian, his Japanese captors tried to break Louis as a way of discouraging resistance among his fellow captives. When he refused to read a propaganda piece for broadcast, they doubled down on the punishment.

But Louis hung on. "Dignity is as essential to human life as water, food, and oxygen," writes Hillenbrand. "The stubborn retention of it, even in the face of extreme physical hardship, can hold a man's soul in his body long past the point at which the body should have surrendered it."[6] At war's end, Louis returned home to a hero's welcome. Not surprisingly, given Hollywood's creeping anti-Christian bias, this is where the movie ends. To be fair, there was too much material in the book for a single movie, but to omit the "Redemption" part promised in the book's subtitle is like showing only the first three quarters of the Super Bowl.

In reality, Louis returned to America with his mind and body unbroken, but his soul ravaged by a PTSD-driven craving for revenge. He suffered recurrent nightmares in which he would be strangling his chief tormentor, in the process waking his wife, Cynthia, and scaring her half to death. To appease his demons, he drank, but that only made things worse.

Cynthia was on the verge of demanding a divorce when a friend talked her into going to hear a fresh young evangelist named Billy Graham. After hearing Graham, she was moved to accept Jesus Christ as her personal savior. To save his marriage, a reluctant Zamperini attended Graham's Crusade as well. Although a believer all his life, he had never fully accepted Jesus. After hearing Graham, however, he was inspired to get down on his knees and open up his heart. "The night I made my decision for Christ," the impressively fit eighty-six-year-old told a Christian interviewer in 2003, "I haven't had a nightmare since."[7]

In 1950, Louis went back to Japan to forgive his captors. "At that moment, something shifted sweetly inside him," writes Hillenbrand. "It was forgiveness, beautiful and effortless and complete. For Louis Zamperini, the war was over."[8] If proof were needed, in 1998, days before his eighty-first birthday, he was still fit enough to run a leg in the torch relay for the Winter Olympics in Japan, not far from the site of his prison camp. He and Cynthia remained happily married until her death in 2001.

In 2018, a year after Louis's death, the Christian film company Pure Flix released *Unbroken: Path to Redemption* to tell the essential part of Louis's story that director Angelina Jolie's big-budget 2014 version chose to omit. True to form, the critics panned it. Nell Minow, writing for RogerEbert. com, spoke of the "criticism from the evangelical community" about the original movie's lack of an ending. She just didn't take that criticism seriously. The sequel, she complained, "has more in common with the low-key aesthetics and overly didactic lessons of Sunday school good-for-you movies than with the more ambitious and wide-ranging original."[9] Ms. Minow was content with the first three quarters of Louis's experience. His fourth quarter comeback held no apparent interest.

Not everyone lives a life like Louis's, but even when not at war or not in training for the Olympics, there is a communal value for men to stay fit. "When you are fit, you are more aware, you care more," says Jack Brewer. "For me, that was my edge. Not just working out. I have to be sound. I have to be sharp."

Wheelchair-bound Tina Hansen discovered this value on a pleasant Tuesday morning in New York City in the fateful year of 2001. Tina was working on the sixty-eighth floor of the World Trade Center's North Tower for the Port Authority when American Airlines Flight 11 slammed into the ninety-third floor. She knew she was in trouble.

Working on the eighty-first floor for a telecommunications company were Mike Benfante, a former college football player now in his mid-thirties, and John Cerqueira, an ultra marathoner. Benfante had recently been hired right out of college. After making sure everyone was evacuated from his floor, Mike followed John down the stairs. Upon reaching the sixty-seventh floor, Mike heard people speaking above him on the sixty-eighth. He and John headed back up and found the door open. Going outside, they saw a group of women huddled around Paine wondering what to do with her.

The men's chivalric impulse kicked in, as did Paine's self-awareness. She knew that after the bombing of the World Trade Center in 1993, management procured some wheelchairs designed to help workers escape future calamities. Mike and John loaded her into one of those chairs and proceeded to carry her in it down sixty-eight flights of stairs, a feat few other men could have pulled off. In instances like this, chivalry has value only to the degree that men are fit enough to fulfill the mission they have chosen for themselves. Fortunately for Tina, these men were.

Mike and John succeeded in clearing Tina from the building and loading her in a waiting ambulance. Ten minutes after the ambulance pulled away, their building, the North Tower, collapsed. The two men took off, not certain they could outrun the dust and debris cloud that followed them up the street. When it caught up with them, the two took cover, and let it pass. As the air cleared, the men found each other and headed uptown together on foot.

On the way down the stairs of the North Tower, Mike and John passed groups of firemen heading up. The firemen took pains to assure those they met that there was nothing to fear and all was under control. From the looks in their eyes, however, John could see that these men sensed they were never coming down. And they did not. Some 343 NYFD firefighters died that day in the line of duty, all of them men. In all, 421 first responders were killed, 418 of them men. "Knowing for most of them that they were entering a building and were never going to come out," said John, "that's not just heroic. That's a demonstration of almost a divinity. It's awe-inspiring, and it represents the best of us."[10]

I do not cite the male-female numbers to make light of the heroic female contribution that day on and behind the front lines. I cite the numbers to shed light on the increasing pressure on fire departments, police departments, the military, and other institutions to ignore the very real physical differences between men and women. Although there are many jobs within the military and police departments that women can perform as well as men, perhaps even better, there is none, really, in fire departments, certainly not on the front lines.

On the website FireRescue1, Alex Bryant breaks down the National Fire Protection Association (NFPA) Standards on fitness. As Bryant notes, "Firefighters need strong aerobic capacity for the rigors of the everyday job, which can include running up stairs, climbing ladders and more. This is all while carrying up to 75 pounds of PPE [personal protective equipment], depending on the job." To assess the potential of would-be firefighters, the NFPA recommends measuring their oxygen consumption, their body mass index, their grip strength, their leg strength, their arm strength, their muscular endurance, and their flexibility. Bryant reminds likely candidates, "Firefighting is a job that requires extraordinary mental and physical fitness."[11] Lives depend on a firefighter's strength and fitness.

Unlike in police departments or the military, the supply of would-be firefighters far exceeds demand, with ratios approaching 100:1 in some cities. Free of political restraints, a big-city fire department could recruit a firefighting corps almost as strong and fit as its NFL team. Given the demand, management could likely find extremely fit firefighters who are also smart, mechanically competent, and good team players.

In the clamor for "inclusion," however, virtually every city government in America is leaning on its fire department to hire more women. In 2019, for instance, the City Council of

New York City amended its administrative code to demand that the NYFD undertake a crash program to recruit more women. This program required recruitment staff, outreach efforts, diversity officers, monitors, and the like. Even greater sums would be spent on permanent firehouse facility upgrades in order to "establish full integration of a mixed gender workforce." This would mean private bathrooms, bunk rooms, locker rooms, and changing areas in each of the city's 254 fire stations.[12] The money spent on administrative overhead and structural repairs will likely be dwarfed in time by the money spent on settling harassment suits, legitimate or otherwise.

None of the money spent on adding women to the department has made New York, a densely populated city of high-rises, any safer. Sixty-three people were killed in NYC fires in 2020. In 2021, fire deaths climbed to seventy-three.[13] In January 2022, seventeen people, including eight children, were killed when a fire ravaged a nineteen-story apartment building in the Bronx section of the city.

Throughout the Western World, gender ideology trumps the safety of the citizenry. As a case in point, New South Wales, in Australia, implemented a quota plan for its Fire and Rescue service that called for a fifty-fifty gender balance in each recruiting class. To protest these quotas anywhere is to kill a career. At the time this plan was under review, the commissioner of the Fire and Rescue NSW, Greg Mullins, put his firefighters on notice. "I am particularly concerned about suggestions that we are dropping standards and employing women incapable of being firefighters." Of course, Mullins was lowering standards, but no one with any ambitions dared say so.

"If you simply don't like working with a more diverse group," Mullins added, "then you need to start looking for a new job."[14]

Firefighting is a dangerous and essential job. Playing in the NFL is a dangerous job, but it is not essential. No citizen has ever died from a dropped pass or a muffed punt. And yet, if an NFL team were forced to abide by the same standards as its city's fire department, the citizenry would burn down city hall. Jack Brewer addressed this issue in my discussion with him. "If you teach kids that men and women are the same," he tells me, "you are going against the order of God." The fact that professional football is allowed to make rational judgments about fitness but fire departments are not tells us just how skewed our values are. Says Brewer, "Being equal before God is what matters."

Women athletes know that men and women are different. In 2017, for instance, a boys' under-fifteen team from Dallas beat the U.S. women's national soccer team 5–2.[15] Only the ideologues were shocked. Unfortunately, the ideologues run many of our institutions, including fire departments. They don't live in run-down nineteen-story buildings chockablock with space heaters, and they apparently don't worry about those who do.

Fit males are an essential part of any well-ordered society. As the history of Rome will attest, to deny them their rightful place in that society is to weaken it. As should be obvious, though, fitness is not a stand-alone virtue for a man. It needs to be tempered by discipline, by the chivalric impulse, ideally by Godliness. When untethered from those other virtues, chaos and heartbreak follow.

Few sports, perhaps none, demand the level of fitness that bicycle racing does. The sport's biggest event, the Tour de France, unfolds over a twenty-three-day period in twenty-one stages covering a total of more than two thousand miles. Riders burn about seven thousand calories a day and lose an average of eleven pounds from their already lean frames over the course of the race.

In the United States, no one personified fitness or resilience the way Lance Armstrong did. An up-and-coming cyclist, Armstrong was sidelined by testicular cancer in 1996. After a two-year struggle, he resumed his career in 1998 and captured the heart of America more completely than any individual competitor since Charles Lindbergh. In 1999, Armstrong won the Tour de France, and he won again each of the next six years. Cancer victims throughout the world looked to him for inspiration. "Without cancer, I never would have won a single Tour de France," said Armstrong. "Cancer taught me a plan for more purposeful living, and that in turn taught me how to train and to win more purposefully."[16]

Unfortunately, that plan did not include God. An outspoken agnostic, Armstrong betrayed his fans, most hurtfully the cancer victims who looked up to him. It was bad enough that he cheated to win by blood doping and using performance-enhancing drugs. Worse was his lying about the use of these illegal techniques. Worst of all was his vicious slander of those who dared to tell the truth. In his race to the top, Armstrong violated just about every principle that an American man should embrace. By sacrificing his honor to win, he lost everything that was dear to him, his reputation first and foremost. "This story was so perfect for so long,"

Armstrong told Oprah Winfrey when he first went public in 2013. "You overcome the disease, you win the Tour de France seven times. You have a happy marriage, you have children. I mean, it's just this mythic perfect story, and it wasn't true."[17] Pride can be a virtue. Hubris never is. If nothing else, Armstrong serves as a useful role model of what the American man is not.

CHAPTER 9

The Married Man

I asked sixteen-year NFL veteran Ben Watson to tell me the most pivotal moment of his life. The star tight end might have said getting drafted in the first round by the New England Patriots or winning the Super Bowl as a rookie.

But no, Ben had a better answer, and he did not hesitate to share it with me. He says simply, "The day I got married." Ben was twenty-four years old at the time. He had met his wife, Kirsten, at a Fellowship of Christian Athletes event while both were students at the University of Georgia. And although he had no doubts about Kirsten, like many young men, Ben was more than a little frightened about what married life held in store. There are few professions, after all, that offer less stability or more temptations than pro football.

His and Kirsten's first three years together were admittedly a little rocky. Ben accepts the lion's share of responsibility for the rough spots. His problem, he came to understand, was his pride. "Pride is our biggest weakness as men," says Ben. With Kirsten's help and support, he worked through it. In time, he came to a critical understanding. "Marriage is not designed to make you happy," he tells me. "Marriage is designed to make you holy."

My parents will not protest if I admit their marriage was not always the prettiest. Like all couples, they have had their ups and downs. But one assurance my mother did have was that my dad would always be there when she needed him. A few years back, she had a serious struggle with lupus. And there was my dad at her side, asserting his will on the hospital staff and making sure they were providing the best care they were capable of. Fortunately, my mother recovered, but she is not sure she would have if it had not been for my dad. After thirty years of marriage, he still takes the "till death do us part" vow seriously.

I asked my friend and former NFL safety Jack Brewer what kind of husband he would like his daughter to choose. Says Jack with a smile, "A man like I am now and not a man like I used to be." He adds, "I trained my daughter to submit to God. I don't want my daughter to submit to a man that doesn't know God."

Although much of this book deals with the relationship between fathers and children, especially fathers and sons, the relationship between a man and his wife deserves special attention. When a man says to a woman, "I promise to be true to you in good times and in bad, in sickness and in health," he makes a vow before God that, if respected, elevates his role in this world. The man seals his commitment with the added promise "I will love you and honor you all the days of my life." Says Brewer, "I don't see how you can be a good husband without God in your life."

When Mike Daly of Staten Island, New York, made this promise to Carol Ann Battaglia in 1964, he had no idea of what would be demanded of him. For years, their life was happy and productive. Mike worked as a New York City police officer, and Carol worked for a bank. They raised three daughters together and would eventually have six grandchildren.

About twenty or so years ago, Mike began to notice Carol's absentmindedness. "And I used to joke about it to my kids," Mike told CBS's chief medical correspondent, Dr. Jonathan LaPook in 2008. "I would say, you know, 'I think she has Alzheimer's, the way she forgets everything.'" Carol was in her late fifties at the time and content with her life. As the memory lapses grew more obvious, she finally went to see a doctor. He confirmed the couple's repressed fears. Carol really did have Alzheimer's.[1]

In 2008, Carol was still cognizant enough to reflect on her future. "I was devastated," said Carol about learning of her diagnosis. "'Cause I saw [Mike's] mother, what she went through. It's terrible. She was walking the streets in the middle of the night. And we had to bring her home." Carol had to give up her job at the bank and suspend many of her household activities. Although a good cook, for instance, she no longer remembered how to make many of the meals she took pride in making. Her illness, though, only brought Mike and Carol closer together.

In 2011, LaPook and a *60 Minutes* crew revisited the Dalys. Carol's condition had continued to deteriorate. By this time, Mike had to help Carol dress and apply her makeup, but he saw this as his chance to repay her for all she had done for him. "She had a job. She cleaned house," said Mike. "She did the wash. She made the beds and she put up with me. So what, what all that's changed for us is the roles. Now I do the wash. I make the beds. I help Carol."

Said LaPook, reflecting perhaps a better understanding of medicine than of marriage, "But that's not what you signed up for?" Answered Mike, "Yes, I did. When you—when we—took our oath, it's for better or for worse. So I did sign up for it in the beginning." Exactly! Although I have yet to make that vow myself, I will have to keep Mike in mind when I do. I will have to ask myself whether I have the will and the honor to do what that man did.

In 2016, when LaPook and *60 Minutes* revisited the Dalys, conversation with Carol was no longer possible. By this point, she was able to do nothing for herself, not even the most basic functions. Mike finally had to reach out for help and hired a home care aide at the cost of almost forty thousand dollars a year. The emotional stress on Mike was even greater than the physical stress. He remembered telling LaPook early in their conversation, "I can handle this," but he did not anticipate the extent of Carol's deterioration. Still, he never gave up trying.

In 2018, with his own health failing and Carol needing twenty-four-hour care, he told LaPook, "I'm coming to the point where maybe a nursing home is, is the answer for her, her safety." Ten days after that conversation and fifty-three years after their wedding day, Mike put Carol in a nursing home. He and Carol had agreed to the *60 Minutes* interviews while Carol was still cognizant as a way to help others prepare for the journey they undertook together. Their struggles were an eye-opener for everyone who watched. Carol died on March 25, 2022, just shy of her seventy-ninth birthday. Mike survived her.

Although Mike and Carol did not take their wedding vows to please the state, they ended up saving the state a small fortune. For more than ten years, Mike and the couple's children freely performed services for Carol that the state would have had to provide if Mike were less honorable or Carol were alone in the world. As their life together attested, the family is the single greatest bulwark against socialism, which is why radical activists want to destroy it. Says Pete Hegseth, who researched this phenomenon for his bestseller, *Battle for the American Mind: Uprooting a Century of Miseducation*, "Traditional families with strong men and strong women and healthy households are a threat to autocrats, are a threat to humanists, are a threat to atheists whose utopian schemes on earth are meant to save us all but always lead to hell."

When thinking of Alzheimer's, many of us think of Ronald Reagan, who spent the last decade or so of his life in its grips. As lovingly as Mike cared for Carol, Reagan's wife, Nancy, cared for him. It was only fitting. While alive and well, there were few more dutiful husbands on the planet than Reagan.

A few days before son Michael Reagan got married in 1971, he received a long and heartfelt letter from his father on the subject of marriage. "You have entered into the most meaningful relationship there is in all human life," Ronald Reagan wrote. "It can be whatever you decide to make it."[2] The future president was writing from experience. His first marriage to actress Jane Wyman had failed. He was likely reflecting on his own experience when he wrote, "The man who puts into the marriage only half of what he owns will get that out."

Michael also saw, however, what happens when a man puts his all into a marriage. At the time of the letter, his father was twenty years into a storybook relationship with Nancy, one that would last for more than fifty years until Ronald's death in 2004. In the letter, Reagan instructed his son on "the challenge of proving your masculinity and charm with one woman for the rest of your life." He focused on fidelity, not just being faithful to a wife but on being so sincerely loving, the wife would have no anxiety at all about sending even a handsome governor and former movie star out into a world of would-be pursuers.

"Any man can find a twerp here and there who will go along with cheating, and it doesn't take all that much manhood. It does take quite a man to remain attractive and to be loved by a woman who has heard him snore, seen him unshaven, tended him while he was sick and washed his dirty underwear," Reagan told his son. "Do that and keep her still feeling a warm glow and you will know some very beautiful music."[3]

The "great communicator," as Reagan was often called, was particularly inspired when speaking of his role as husband. No one who knew him and Nancy and had seen them together doubted his sincerity. "There is no greater happiness for a man," concluded Reagan at the end of the letter to Michael, "than approaching a door at the end of a day knowing someone on the other side of that door is waiting for the sound of his footsteps."[4] That marriage, Nancy's one and only, proved to be the bedrock on which Reagan built his political career, a career that would see Reagan emerge as the most successful president in the twentieth century. He never failed to thank Nancy for making it happen.

On the occasion of Christmas 1981, nine months after Reagan had been shot and nearly killed, he put his thoughts about Nancy down in writing. On the occasion of Nancy's death in 2016, former Canadian Prime Minister Brian Mulroney read the letter at her funeral.[5] In the letter, Reagan discussed the many sides of Nancy's character. "There is of course my 'First Lady,'" he said. "She brings so much grace and charm to whatever she does that even stuffy, formal functions sparkle and turn into fun times."

Reagan next addresses Nancy's compassionate side, one that the world rarely saw. "She takes an abandoned child in her arms on a hospital visit," he observed. "The look on her face only the Madonna could match. The look on the child's face is one of adoration. I know because I adore her too." Then, too, there was the nest builder. "If she were stuck three days in a hotel room," Reagan joked, "she'd manage to make it home sweet home." He adored the cowgirl as well. Said

Reagan, "She's a wonderful person to sit by the fire with, or to ride with or first to be with when the sun goes down or the stars come out."

Although sentimental, Nancy "loves to laugh and her laugh is like tinkling bells. I hear those bells and feel good all over even if I tell a joke she's heard before." Concluded the president, "Fortunately, all these women in my life are you— fortunately for me that is, for there could be no life for me without you." Nancy felt the same. "Everything just fell into place," she told an interviewer. "We completed each other."[6]

Here Nancy was expressing a thought as old as Judeo-Christian culture. In Genesis, we are told that God created for man a companion that was, as Adam said, "bone of my bones and flesh of my flesh." This rightly ordered sexual relationship was essential for human flourishing, and it was to serve as the model for all those going forward. "Therefore," Genesis 2:24 tells us, "a man shall leave his father and mother and be joined to his wife, and they shall become one flesh."

"The two become one," Ben Watson reminds me, "and the 'one' creates a new one." In the Watsons' case, the one created seven new ones and two additional children lost to miscarriage. "A kid deserves two parents," says Ben.

Although there are any number of books available on marriage, the one that I have found most helpful is Gary Chapman's *The 5 Love Languages for Men*. I am obviously not the only one who feels this way. Chapman, a trained theologian, has sold multiple millions of copies in the "5 Love Languages" series in upward of fifty different languages. His success is not hard to understand. He speaks directly and succinctly to the challenges all men face, even those of us not yet married.

Chapman begins with the premise that "the need to feel loved by one's spouse is at the heart of marital desires." This need is as true of men as it is of women. In his "Men" book, he puts the burden on the man to understand how best to communicate with the woman in his life. He notes, "Everyone has a primary love language—a way of expressing devotion and affection that touches us deep inside, occasionally puts a goofy grin on our face, and leaves no doubt that we are truly and spectacularly loved."[7]

Chapman envisions five ways to communicate love. These are the "love languages." Some, like "words of affirmation," are more obvious than others, for instance, "acts of service." The others are "quality time," "gift giving," and "physical touch." In looking at a relationship like the Reagans', we can see each of the partners communicating openly and freely in all five languages.

Although most couples fall short of that ideal, Chapman believes that every man has the capability of being at least bilingual. He can communicate his love in the language that he knows best—like, say, fixing a leaky faucet—but he must understand his mate well enough to speak in the language most instinctive to her, whether it is receiving gifts or compliments or spending time together or touching.

"When you express your love for your wife using her primary love language," Chapman writes in a language men can understand, "it's like hitting the sweet spot on a baseball bat or golf club. It just feels right—and the results are impressive."[8]

At the core of all five languages is the element of sacrifice. A man must discipline himself to do something he would not instinctively do to please the woman in his life.

This sacrifice may cost him time he values for other activities or money he might otherwise spend on his own pleasures. When I read about a man like Mike Daly, I am blown away by the sacrifices he made to care for his wife, Carol. As her faculties diminished, he adapted his love languages accordingly. Words of affirmation went unheard, but touch never lost its value. Mike's love was so transcendent, in fact, he persisted in caring for Carol even after she was deaf to all of the love languages, except maybe touch.

A loving husband, Chapman argues, should work not only to speak his wife's love language, but also to refrain from using language that hurts her. I don't think that I go out on a limb here to say that women are easily hurt. Anger may be a natural response to many circumstances, Chapman notes, but "verbal or physical explosions that attack the other person are not appropriate responses to anger."[9]

Chapman suggests simple ways to remediate an explosive situation, but these do not come easily to any of us, no matter how simple—for instance, apologizing. "Done well, an apology can bring closure to tensions, conflicts, and hurt feelings that have been sore spots for months, even years," writes Chapman. "It can change the way your wife thinks of you—the way she looks at you. It can break down barriers faster than any other words or actions can." Three one-syllable words, "I was wrong," can heal a world of hurt.[10]

Comedian Jeff Foxworthy has made an extraordinarily successful career for himself presenting similar instructions on being a good husband, but with an obvious comic twist. Those who want a short course on the subject might profitably check out Jeff Foxworthy's "The Rules of Marriage" on YouTube.[11]

In a more serious moment, Foxworthy sat down with Pastor J to discuss his own marriage. "We all want to receive grace," said Foxworthy. "We're much stingier about giving it away." As to specific advice, Foxworthy volunteered, "Looking at [your wives] the way you looked at them when you were dating." The deeply Christian Foxworthy may be fluent in other love languages, but when it comes to "words of affirmation," he is a natural. "I've been married thirty-six years," he told Pastor J. "I don't think I've ever had a day that I haven't at least once during the day said to my wife, 'Has anyone told you [that you] are the prettiest girl in the world?'"[12]

Not yet married myself, I take great heart from those who have been married long and well. Nearing his twentieth wedding anniversary, Ben Watson sums up its possibilities: "Marriage is better than advertised when done in humility before God."

CHAPTER 10

Man as Provider

Although the 2006 Matthew McConaughey film *Failure to Launch* did not win any major awards or set the box office on fire, it did provide psychologists a new name for an old syndrome, namely the reluctance of young men to leave home and form their own families. "When young adults stay at home, don't search for a job or contribute financially, and begin to withdraw from the world, we have the foundation of failure to launch," writes Ellen Hendriksen in *Scientific American*. "Add unrealistic goals, blaming others for their situation, and a lack of motivation to change, and liftoff is almost sure to be grounded."[1]

The syndrome was widespread enough to earn a name before the COVID-19 outbreak, but in the years since, it has become its own pandemic. The lockdown provided cultural support to those young males disinclined to support themselves in the first place. Forced to return to their parents' homes from closed college campuses or small apartments in jobless big cities, the newly grounded joined the never launched to form a cultural bloc of their own.

Psychologists have cited any number of reasons for the phenomenon, and mental illness may be one part of the equation, but the larger reason why young males retreat like this is because they can. The nation is prosperous enough, and parents are indulgent enough, that a young person can live comfortably in a household, usually with a room of his own, without contributing to its support. This prosperity extends even to homes relying on public assistance. In America, there is more than enough to go around, maybe too much.

Despite their good intentions, parents contribute to the syndrome by demanding too little of children old enough to vote. Too often, they prepare their meals, clean their clothes, and lend them money. In the last several years, even during the pandemic, low-end jobs have gone begging because young people lack the motivation to take them. In addition to the parents, the government has stepped in to keep these young people comfortably idle. Left to their own devices, unemployed or underemployed young males turn too often to a subsidized life of mindless video games, social media, pornography, and drugs. Indeed, as many as a hundred thousand people are dying each year of fentanyl and other drugs with the average victims being young and male with an ethnic profile not unlike that of the United States as a whole.

Sean Hannity has a difficult time understanding this phenomenon. Hannity cites two things that have kept him grounded throughout his life: his Catholic faith and hard work. Like me, Hannity learned the value of work from his parents. Born in Brooklyn's Bedford-Stuyvesant to an immigrant mother who died during childbirth, Sean's father, Hugh, never stopped working. Neither, for that matter, did Sean's mother, Lillian.

A World War II veteran, Hugh worked during the week as a probation officer. On weekends, he worked as a waiter. Although valedictorian of her high school class, Lillian could not afford college and became a correction officer at a county jail because the job paid better than did stenography. Between them, they saved enough to move the family from the mean streets of Brooklyn to Hempstead on Long Island, where Sean and his three older sisters grew up. What extra money Hugh and Lillian made paid for the Catholic education of their children.

As a kid coming up, Sean always worked. He had a paper route before moving into the restaurant business, there progressing from dishwasher to busboy to waiter to bartender. "I loved sports and making money," Sean tells me. He saved enough to send himself to college for two years, but his interest waned as the money ran out. In the summers between semesters, he discovered his aptitude for building. After leaving college, he moved full-time into construction work and mastered a full range of skills—from painting to paperhanging to laying tile to framing houses. Not until he was twenty-eight and working as a general contractor did Sean take his first stab at radio and then as a volunteer. Thirty-three years later, he is still going strong.

"It was ingrained in my DNA to be a provider," Sean tells me. "That was my job." The father of two grown children, Sean has provided for his family in great style in no small part because he was willing to outwork everyone else. Although critics have mocked him for not having a college degree, Sean attributes his success as a broadcaster less to any natural gift than to an ability to understand what will resonate with working people. For ten years or more, he made his living with his hands. He can relate to his audience's everyday struggles, but the failure-to-launch generation still mystifies him. "I never met a man who was supported by someone else who was satisfied with his life," he says.

The failure to form a meaningful relationship with a woman is one reason a male may remain poor and dependent on the state or on his parents. For all the talk of wage gaps, the one real and enduring wage gap is between single males and married men. Analysts may disagree on why this is so, but there is no denying that married men make on average as much as one-third more than their single peers. The obvious reason for this is that a working wife gives her husband more freedom to explore the job market. If the wife handles the bulk of domestic duties, this also frees the man to work longer hours.

A deeper reason is that women often encourage their husbands to fulfill their potential. "My wife is the one who tells me you can do it," says Ben Watson. "She is the reason why I have tried to do half the things I've done." Then, too, Watson adds, "Many of my bad habits were broken because of her."

There is still another reason behind the married man's productivity. And that is, since the beginning of time, men have felt an instinctive need to support their wives and children. God made Eve the mother of all humanity, but the responsibility for their fate God laid on Adam. As noted in Genesis 3:17, "Because you have heeded the voice of your wife, and have eaten from the tree of which I commanded you, saying, 'You shall not eat of it': Cursed *is* the ground for your sake; In toil you shall eat *of* it, All the days of your life."

Virtually all cultures warn against idleness. In one of his fables from about twenty-six hundred years ago, Aesop told the tale of the grasshopper who sang and danced the summer away while his ant friend worked to store up food for the winter. When winter came, the grasshopper went begging for food, but the ant rebuked him for his idleness and turned him away. The grasshopper's failure to launch came at a high price. Ants like myself who have not yet married see the period before marriage as a time to store up resources for the family to come. As you might expect, not all single workingmen my age are ants. Nightclubs and strip bars would go out of business if they were.

Working hard comes with rewards, some incalculable. Ever since Adam, men have taken great satisfaction in being able to provide for their wives and children. This instinct has been preserved in nursery rhymes at least three centuries old, for instance, "Bye, baby Bunting / Daddy's gone a-hunting / Gone to get a rabbit skin / To wrap the baby Bunting in." The satisfaction comes through individual initiative. When a larger collective takes away from the individual the responsibility for the work and the rewards that follow, the result is never good and often disastrous.

America dodged a nearly lethal bullet four hundred years ago when Plymouth Governor William Bradford had the good sense to abandon a scheme that wreaked havoc on his struggling colony. Bradford had arrived on the *Mayflower* with his fellow British refugees looking for a land in which they could practice their brand of Christianity in peace. Schoolchildren may know about the Pilgrims' first Thanksgiving, but even their teachers know little or nothing about the group's flirtation with socialism.

The Pilgrims, Bradford observes, made a misjudgment not unlike that of Adam and Eve in aspiring to a wisdom reserved for God. He tells the story of their folly in his journal *Of Plymouth Plantation*. "The experience that was had in this common course and condition, tried sundry years and that amongst godly and sober men," he writes, "may well evince the vanity of that conceit of Plato's and other ancients applauded by some of later times; that the taking away of property and bringing in community into a commonwealth would make them happy and flourishing; as if they were wiser than God." This scheme, although entered voluntarily, worked out no better than it would for Stalin or Mao or Pol Pot. It flouted human nature, in Bradford's words[2]:

> For this community (so far as it was) was found to breed much confusion and discontent and retard much employment that would have been to their benefit and comfort. For the young men, that were most able and

fit for labour and service, did repine that they should spend their time and strength to work for other men's wives and children without any recompense. The strong, or man of parts, had no more in division of victuals and clothes than he that was weak and not able to do a quarter the other could; this was thought injustice.

The aged and graver men to be ranked and equalized in labours and victuals, clothes, etc., with the meaner and younger sort, thought it some indignity and disrespect unto them. And for men's wives to be commanded to do service for other men, as dressing their meat, washing their clothes, etc., they deemed it a kind of slavery, neither could many husbands well brook it. Upon the point all being to have alike, and all to do alike, they thought themselves in the like condition, and one as good as another; and so, if it did not cut off those relations that God hath set amongst men, yet it did at least much diminish and take off the mutual respects that should be preserved amongst them. And would have been worse if they had been men of another condition.

Bradford rejected the idea that the experiment failed because the people of Plymouth were ill suited to it. "Let none object this is men's corruption, and nothing to the course itself," he writes. "I answer, seeing all men have this corruption in them, God in His wisdom saw another course fitter for them." Bradford and his fellows promptly took that other course. After much debate, "The Governor (with the advice of the chiefest amongst them) gave way that they should set corn every man for his own particular, and in that regard trust to themselves."

The experiment in collective work came to an end. The return to individual property and self-reliance "made all hands very industrious, so as much more corn was planted than otherwise would have been by any means the Governor or any other could use, and saved him a great deal of trouble, and gave far better content." It was not just the men who worked harder. "The women," Bradford notes, "now went willingly into the field, and took their little ones with them to set corn; which before would allege weakness and inability; whom to have compelled would have been thought great tyranny and oppression."

If Bradford and the Pilgrims were able to resolve the tension between collectivism and responsible individualism in their community, that tension has not been resolved in the Black community. "Why do we cling to an adversarial, victim-focused identity that preoccupies us with white racism?" asks Black author Shelby Steele. "I think this identity is a weight on blacks because it is built around our collective insecurity rather than in our faith in our human capacity to seize opportunity as individuals. It amounts to a self-protective collectivism that obsesses us with black unity instead of individual initiative."[3]

I think we see increasingly in today's failure-to-launch generation the same corruptive effect that collective thinking had on the young men in Bradford's generation as well as on those young men raised in a welfare culture. Knowing their basic needs will be met in any case, the young don't see the need to work any harder than anyone else is working. Their tendency toward sloth is reinforced by an educational establishment that has managed to convince more than half of young adults that socialism is a good thing.[4] Ignorance of history is a necessary ingredient in repeating it.

One person that educators did not convince was Chris Gardner. Gardner listened instead to his "old-fashioned" mother who told him every single day, "Son, you can do or be anything that you want to do or be." Says Gardner, "I believed it. I bought into it 100%." Gardner related his own story in his memoir, *The Pursuit of Happyness*, later made into a 2006 movie of the same name starring Will Smith as Gardner. The title refers, of course, to one of the three pillars of America's foundation—life and liberty being the other two. Born in 1954 into a fatherless Milwaukee family, Gardner had the "pursuit of happiness" gene baked into his very American DNA. I believe we all do, in fact, which is why educators have to work so hard to extricate it.

After service in the U.S. Navy, Gardner returned to the real world with a passion to succeed. His life as a young man was a little messier than the one portrayed in the movie, but what was entirely genuine was his drive to provide for his young son. "I made a decision as a five-year-old boy that my kids will know who their father is," Gardner told a BBC interviewer.[5] As he struggled to gain a footing in the business world, he and Chris Jr. spent a year essentially homeless, spending nights in shelters and BART station bathrooms. The need to provide reinforced his own inherent drive.

In real life, as in the film, Gardner worked relentlessly to become a stockbroker at Dean Witter Reynolds in San

Francisco. Lacking connections, he had to earn his keep by making cold calls, hundreds of them a day to secure the few that would pay the bills. Although society has a tendency to dismiss the work of salesmen, Gardner knew better. "Salespeople are the most important people in any organization," he says with some accuracy. "Until a salesperson gets an order, nobody in the company has a job."[6] Gardner's hard work and persistence paid off, and he eventually started his own firm.

Gardner has parlayed his success story into a lucrative career as a motivational speaker, his fees ranging upward of fifty thousand dollars an appearance. He has been particularly eloquent in addressing America's young. In a short video titled "The Speech Every Student Must Hear," he acknowledges the defeatism that confronts youth at every turn, the messaging that tells them, "The sky is falling." His experience has given him another perspective. Counters Gardner, "I will say those are pennies from heaven."[7]

Gardner's "new vision of the American dream" transcends wealth. It is as old as the Declaration of Independence, older even. Its roots are in the Gospels. The Founding Fathers took political philosopher John Locke's ideas on the "pursuit of property" and transformed them to the more expansive "pursuit of happiness." The founders may have recognized that for a nation founded on Christian ideals, there is more to life than property. After a career of sometimes desperate striving, Gardner has certainly come to believe this. "Achieving balance in your life," he tells young people, "is more important than achieving the balance in your checking account."

Gardner uses the metaphor of Joseph Campbell's monomyth to explain a man's role in life. He sees man not so much as an "earner" but as a "provider." Says Gardner, "For too long a lot of us have been exiled in a place called things. And it's time for us to come home to friends, families, and folks." The idea of coming home is critical to the understanding of what makes a man.

The late Jeffrey Epstein certainly made a lot of money, but if you do an internet search for "Epstein" and "children," you are not going to read about his offspring. You are going to read about his victims. When he died at sixty-six, he left behind no spouse and no children, at least none officially recognized. In his "place called things," young females were "the things." His case is extreme, but his lifestyle was not.

The man who popularized that lifestyle, Hugh Hefner, died in 2017, two years before Epstein did. Hefner left behind a veritable empire of things. The title of his magazine, *Playboy*, unintentionally captured the immaturity of the males it appealed to. These were "boys," not "men." For these boys, Hefner glorified material acquisition—cars, liquor, clothes—with no finer acquisition than a "trophy" wife or, better yet, girlfriend. For a playboy with aspirations like Hefner, the ultimate trophy was the "playmate of the month," with the emphasis on "play."

Missouri Senator Josh Hawley is one of the few elected officials to speak truth to this corrupting power. Like Gardner, he asked the young men in his audience to "aspire to be something more than a consumer," especially a consumer of pornography. Too many youth are "too despairing," Hawley told Fox News's Tucker Carlson, a message Hawley had delivered a few days earlier at AmFest. "The truth is that what the porn industry is selling them is a total lie." For a young man, said Hawley, "the single greatest act of rebellion" against today's prevailing liberal culture is "to go out and actually engage in real relationships, get married, have a family, have kids, have your own ideas and be a responsible member of society." Added Hawley, "This is what people are built to do. This is what young people want to do."[8] They want to provide. They want to create. And short of a cure for cancer, the greatest creation any man leaves behind is a sound and healthy extended family.

In the Western World today, not enough people are doing what Hawley recommends—getting married, having children, and providing for those children. The 2022 birth rate in the United States is a little more than half of what it was in 1960, and it is well below replacement level. Even Democratic Senate leader Chuck Schumer has acknowledged the shortfall of new Americans. Said Schumer in November 2022 outside the Capitol, "Now more than ever, we're short of workers. We have a population that is not reproducing on its own with the same level that it used to."[9]

The fact that his party's policies have led to the abortion of more than sixty million potential "workers" over the previous fifty years did not seem to enter Schumer's thinking. Instead of encouraging Americans to marry and have children, he encouraged the continuing flow of illegal immigration. "The only way we're going to have a great future in America is if we welcome and embrace immigrants, the Dreamers and—all of them."

America has a long, if imperfect, history of welcoming immigrants. Legal immigration begins with the understanding that the new arrivals will be able to provide for themselves or be provided for by their American relatives. People who arrive illegally have no such expectation and little chance of creating and sustaining their own independent families. Schumer and his allies know this. They do not want productive, free-thinking new citizens. They want dependent "workers."

Conservative observers were quick to note the irony. It was hard not to. Said political strategist Greg Price, "They say that it's empowering to stay single forever and never start a family, claim having kids destroys the environment, promote abortion as a moral good, and their solution when they realize people aren't having enough kids is to import the third world to replace them."[10]

Despite the lack of "workers," many of those who support Schumer's policies have an open contempt for those American citizens who have more than two children and who support those children on their own. Popular blogger Lisa Lewis discovered the depth of this contempt when she posted a photo of her pregnant self with her husband and their four small children. "So I don't usually publicly address the Negative Nancys and Pouty Pauls that find it necessary to judge my life choices," said Lewis on Instagram. "BUT a number of ppl have been commenting and even having the nerve to send me DM's regarding my pregnancy…'I thought y'all was done?' 'How can y'all afford 5?' Listen here! I am a married, ADULT! I have one baby daddy."

Lewis felt the need to speak out because of the media depiction of parents of color as "incapable of raising large families positively." This is true enough, but the resistance to large families crosses color lines. "I just want you to know that white people do get criticized for having lots of kids," one friendly fan replied. "I have six and people have said the most unbelievably rude things TO MY FACE. I don't have a platform like you do to try and affect change, but I am so glad people like you stand up and take charge with issues people have no business weighing in on!" Lewis concluded her post on a positive note. "I feel super blessed that Joe and I work (very hard)," said Lewis. "We are a parental UNIT, and we work hard to provide and raise good people."[11] Hats off to Joe. America needs more men like him—many more.

Dr. Lauren Miller adds an interesting wrinkle to the discussion of man as provider. Although the man's first responsibility is to provide "security" in the way of a home, an income, safety, and the like, "A great man," she adds, "is also able to be an emotional provider." By this, Miller means that the man provides the comfort and relief that all women need to "recharge the battery." This emotional support, says Miller, "makes everything so much easier."

Dr. Miller seems to be describing former NFL defensive end Devon Still. In June 2014, while still working to secure his position with the Cincinnati Bengals, his life took a dramatic turn. His four-year-old daughter, Leah, was diagnosed with neuroblastoma, stage 4 cancer. "The easiest decision I ever made," he tells me, was to be there for his daughter. He spent the next three weeks sleeping by her side at the hospital. "I had to show her she meant more than football."

In the next few years, Still showed how the seemingly contradictory strains of traditional masculinity could be resolved if the will was there to resolve them. The most obvious conflict centered on his role as provider and his role as protector. If he put football aside to protect Leah, he jeopardized his ability to provide for her and his fiancée, Asha. His father taught him, however, to fight adversity and to push through life's struggles. He was not about to abandon Leah and her mom.

As a responsible father, Still made his decision to stay easier by having "put money in the bank." Just as important, he had an employer who actually cared. Bengals head coach Marvin Lewis offered Still a position on the practice squad. In this way, he would continue to receive health benefits but would not have to travel with the team. The Bengals, in fact, supported Still and his family throughout the ordeal.

The trickier conflict pitted his deeply ingrained resistance to show emotion with Leah's need for him to be what Dr. Miller called an "emotional provider." Like most men, Still had grown up learning not to cry. This training has merit. Men who break down, say, when their car breaks down have little value to their families. Crying when you are bullied or your wife is threatened does no one any good. But, as Still learned, when your cancer-stricken daughter tells you she is shielding her pain because you show no emotion, it is time to reevaluate the limits of emotional control. "I cried on TV," he tells me, "because people needed to see what the struggle was like."

The venue where Still showed his emotions most publicly was at the ESPY Awards, the same event at which Jim Valvano made his memorable speech. As Valvano conceded during that speech, "I'm a very emotional, passionate man." He continued with a smile, "I can't help it, that's being the son of Rocco and Angelina Valvano. It comes with the territory, right? We hug, we kiss, we love."

Like me and most other American men, Still did not grow up that way. He had to learn to let his emotions show when the time was right to show them. In accepting the Jimmy V Perseverance Award, the six-foot-five, three-hundred-pound Still concluded his speech with a poignant tribute to Leah, then still deep in her battle to survive.

I just want to thank you. From the moment you was born you molded me into the man I am today. And you know I always used to dream about how I was going to be able to show you so much about life. But in the five years I've been with you you've taught me more about life than I could ever do. I love you and I'm just proud of the way you've been handling yourself this past year.

At the speech's end, a roomful of the biggest, baddest, toughest athletes in America quietly wiped away their tears. Devon and Asha married in 2016. As of this writing, Leah remains cancer-free, and she loves her two new sisters.

CHAPTER 11

The Knowledgeable Man

For the last thirty-five years, one television character above all others has endured as the prototypical American male. I refer here, of course, to our favorite nuclear safety inspector, Springfield's own Homer Simpson, the *pater familias* of the long-running show *The Simpsons*.

I would not take the Homer character seriously if he were the exception to the rule, but he is not. He is the norm. Homer subverts the work ethic—"Son, if you really want something in this life, you have to work for it. Now quiet! They're about to announce the lottery numbers." He disparages education—"How is education supposed to make me feel smarter? Besides, every time I learn something new, it pushes some old stuff out of my brain." He undermines individual initiative—"Trying is the first step towards failure." And much too often to be coincidental, he mocks people of faith—"I was working on a flat tax proposal and I accidentally proved there's no god."[1]

As I sit here thinking about my own exposure to popular culture, I can think of lots of dolts like Simpson, but I am hard pressed to conjure a recurring image of a competent, knowledgeable male character. The media are equally stingy in elevating real-life wise men. In the way of a thought exercise, finish the following jibe: "Yeah, you're a genius. You're a regular _____!" I find myself saying "Einstein."

The only problem is that Albert Einstein, the great German-born physicist, died thirty-five years before I was born. Throughout recorded history, in all cultures, wisdom has been valued, and the wise man celebrated. The Bible gives us Solomon, not to mention Jesus and the Apostle Paul. The Greek tradition honored many of its great intellectuals—Socrates, Plato, and Aristotle among others. The Romans did the same for Cicero and Marcus Aurelius, as did the early Christians with Augustine and later Thomas Aquinas. This recognition of wise men continued throughout the Western World, America included, but seems to have reached a dead end with Einstein.

Part of the problem is ideological. Consider the five cases that follow, four current, one more than a century old. These cases resonate with me as an American and, more directly, as a Black American. The first involves Booker T. Washington, one of my personal heroes. His 1901 memoir, *Up from Slavery*, first serialized in a Christian newspaper, still resonates with me. Born into slavery in 1856, Washington turned nine just four days before General Robert E. Lee surrendered, effectively ending the Civil War. Now free to learn, Washington eagerly did just that, teaching himself to read and reading every book he could get his hands on.

To pay for a higher education, Washington worked in West Virginia's coal mines and salt furnaces. He saved enough to attend what is now known as Hampton University and later Virginia Union University. In 1881, Lewis Adams, a former slave, and George Campbell, a former slave owner, collaborated to establish the Tuskegee Normal School for Colored Teachers in Alabama. Needing someone to lead the school, the pair reached out to the Hampton Institute for a recommendation. Hampton administrators suggested one of its brightest scholars, Booker T. Washington, despite the fact that he was not yet twenty-five years old.

The philosophy that Washington would famously share with his largely White audience at Atlanta's Cotton States and International Exposition of 1895, he had been implementing since day one at Tuskegee. To prosper, he told the Atlanta audience, a man—any man—must "learn to dignify and glorify common labour, and put brains and skill into the common occupations of life."[2] At Tuskegee, Washington had the students helping to build the Institute from day one. His goal was not just to save on labor costs but also to instruct his students in the building crafts, a knowledge base that still has value to this day. In addition, Washington developed a large farm on campus and had his students work it, again both for institutional sustainability and for student enrichment. As Washington observed in Atlanta, "No race can prosper till it learns that there is as much dignity in tilling a field as in writing a poem."

A point that Washington made at Atlanta is one that I have made elsewhere in the book, namely that "when it comes to business, pure and simple, it is in the South that the Negro is given a man's chance in the commercial world." For all the barriers thrown up to civic and social equality in the Jim Crow South, the concept of free enterprise remained, as it should be everywhere, largely free. To exploit that potential, Washington offered some advice that makes even more sense today than it did then, encouraging his Black audience not to "permit our grievances to overshadow our opportunities."

For Washington, the keys to progress were skill and knowledge. He had little use for unearned titles or empty credentials. The pitch he made at Atlanta was that Black progress was good for the White South as well. "There is no defense or security for any of us except in the highest intelligence and development of all," he argued. "We shall constitute one-third and more of the ignorance and crime of the South, or one-third [of] its intelligence and progress."

In citing the fact that Blacks comprised just one-third of the South's population, Washington acknowledged that he was not speaking from a position of strength. Whites not only had greater numbers, but also had much greater resources. He had long ago made the strategic decision to appeal to the better angels of his White compatriots. He thought this a wiser policy than to demand what he called the "artificial forcing" of social equality. "No race that has anything to contribute to the markets of the world," he said, "is long in any degree ostracized."

To illustrate the wisdom of Washington's thinking, all we need do is reflect on the dining choices available in any American city today. If White supremacy really ruled the land, and the WASP establishment imposed its hegemonic control over our daily lives, we would all be eating peas and Brussels sprouts at our local British restaurant. But we're not. We are eating at those ethnic restaurants whose food tastes the best. In this fight for market share, seemingly disfavored groups such as the Chinese, the Mexicans, and the Italians have clearly outperformed more seemingly favored groups such as the British, the Germans, and the Scandinavians. I like a good Danish as much as anyone, but I've never been to a Danish restaurant, let alone an English one. Black Americans have had more success than some ethnic groups in finding a market for their food, but not as much success as others. In other areas of endeavor—music and sports most obviously—Blacks have, as they say, punched well above their weight.

A lot of my philosophy comes from Booker T. Washington as reinforced by my father: Do not wait for the government to do what we can do for ourselves; the ball is now in our court; do not expect anyone to save us. My dad does not believe, as many in the Black community still do, that Blacks have to work twice as hard to get half as far. That maxim was likely true in Washington's time. My father is a realist. All he asked is that we work our hardest, and everything else would sort itself out. "No matter who your opponent," he would tell me, "beat their ass." My dad didn't waste words.

I took that advice to heart. When people ask how I have gotten to where I am at age thirty, I tell them that I am constantly competing with myself to fulfill my potential. From time to time, I have to channel my inner Booker T. and reignite that hunger to be the best. It surprises me to see so many young people from all backgrounds who content themselves with doing just enough to get by, and sometimes not even that.

Black America has been particularly vulnerable to this malaise. For all the successes of the larger Black community, I suspect that if Booker T. Washington were alive today, he would not be pleased by the progress among the less affluent half of the Black population. Our educational establishment has pushed academic credentials, often at the expense of real-world knowledge and marketable skills, and young men of lesser means have been too often left behind as a result.

What I am sure would please Washington are the recent moves by Clifford Joseph Harris Jr.—the rapper, actor, and fashion impresario better known as "T.I." A street tough with multiple arrests as an adolescent, Harris transformed his life through his commitment to his music. He then parlayed his initial success as a performer into production and other entrepreneurial ventures.

Partnering with fellow rapper "Killer Mike" and some other investors, Harris is buying back his old neighborhood and redeveloping it without government subsidies. "But I didn't want it to be one of those situations where luxury condos go up, and people who are native are pushed out to the fringes because they can't afford to live there," Harris told *Inc.* Magazine. "I wanted to provide development that would allow people from the area, who love the community, to be able to afford to stay."[3]

This effort strikes me as a manifestation of Washington's philosophy in action. That it is happening in Atlanta seems altogether fitting, especially given, as shall be seen, the abuse Washington received for the so-called "Atlanta Compromise." Even in Washington's day, however, entrepreneurial success was within reach of Black Americans. When educators deign to mention this fact, however, they almost inevitably place it in its most negative context, specifically the destruction of Tulsa's "Black Wall Street" in a deadly 1921 pogrom.

That horror had much the same motivation as the pogroms that drove Jews out of Eastern Europe, in this case "white animosity against black economic progress." The problem in Tulsa was not free enterprise. Blacks did impressively well there, owning hotels, banks, movie theaters, clothiers, cafés, and the like. The problem was human nature. No matter what their motivation, mobs are the natural enemy of the rule of law, the very oxygen that sustains free enterprise everywhere.[4]

In 1901, Washington dined with President Theodore Roosevelt in the White House. This was the first highly publicized meeting of a Black man with a president as equals or something like it. Having met with President Trump myself, I can safely say that the president always has the home court advantage in such meetings, no matter whom he meets. For Washington, Tuskegee was home. In 1915, when he fell ill with nephritis in New York City, he insisted on boarding a train for Tuskegee, the Institute he had spent the last thirty-five years building. He died a few hours after arriving, at age fifty-nine.

Even before his death, however, Washington had generated a fair amount of criticism within the Black community. Leading the charge against Washington's strategy of self-reliance and accommodation was the activist intellectual W. E. B. Du Bois. Born just a dozen years later than Washington, William Edward Burghardt Du Bois grew up in a different world. He spent his early years in integrated Massachusetts schools, earned a doctorate from Harvard, and cofounded the NAACP in 1909.

Initially, Du Bois praised Washington's Atlanta speech, calling it "the basis for a real settlement between whites and black in the South." By the time of his 1903 book, *The Souls of Black Folk*, Du Bois was denouncing the speech as the "Atlanta Compromise." By taking a scalpel to Washington and not a broadsword, Du Bois made a compelling case that the strategy "has tended to make the whites, North and South, shift the burden of the Negro problem to the Negro's shoulders and stand aside as critical and rather pessimistic spectators." Du Bois argued instead that "the burden belongs to the nation, and the hands of none of us are clean if we bend not our energies to righting these great wrongs."[5]

Du Bois lobbied for the cultivation of what he called the "Talented Tenth," the upper 10 percent of the Black male population—the "exceptional men"—that would, in the language of the time, save the Negro race. A century or so ago, higher education apparently offered more content than it does today:

> If we make money the object of man-training, we shall
> develop money-makers but not necessarily men; if we

make technical skill the object of education, we may possess artisans but not, in nature, men. Men we shall have only as we make manhood the object of the work of the schools—intelligence, broad sympathy, knowledge of the world that was and is, and of the relation of men to it—this is the curriculum of that Higher Education which must underlie true life.[6]

Despite their differing strategies, both Washington and Du Bois saw knowledge as the path to power. Du Bois, in fact, equated knowledge with manliness. I suspect that he would have a hard time making that equation today were he to visit an American university. The academic celebration of gender fluidity, safe spaces, and speech codes would appall a scholar like Du Bois, who saw free speech and open debate as the birthright of every man.

Du Bois addressed the free speech issue in his critique of Booker T. Washington. As he noted, Washington's reputation was so strong and his influence so vast that many Americans, White and Black, were hesitant to challenge his program. Ironically, in the university today, those most likely to take the Du Bois side in a debate are the ones most likely to silence their opponents. The openly leftist Du Bois capped his flirtation with communism by joining the Communist Party USA in 1961, two years before his death. His woke heirs on our campuses need to read Du Bois's take on tactics like theirs:

But the hushing of the criticism of honest opponents is a dangerous thing. It leads some of the best of the critics to unfortunate silence and paralysis of effort, and others to burst into speech so passionately and intemperately as to lose listeners. Honest and earnest criticism from those whose interests are most nearly touched,—criticism of writers by readers, of government by those governed, of leaders by those led,—this is the soul of democracy and the safeguard of modern society.[7]

In a more open society, we would be celebrating the lives and careers of both Washington and Du Bois, two extraordinary men of knowledge. "Honest and earnest criticism" might compel some to challenge Washington's conservatism and others to challenge Du Bois's communism, but the resulting dialogue would prove beneficial for everyone willing to listen.

Unfortunately, "conservative" anything has almost no place on the American campus today. As popular "antiracist" intellectual Ta-Nehisi Coates argued in *The Atlantic*, "Washington's 'Atlanta Compromise' is remembered as a betrayal and a sell-out because it accepted segregation, and argued against black political agitation."[8] When Washington does show up in curricula, students are usually asked to contrast his philosophy with that of Du Bois and others. I am sure there are teachers somewhere that give Washington a fair shake, but I just cannot imagine there are many of them.

The talented tenth of Black Americans are doing just fine today, maybe even the talented half. Had Washington's strategy prevailed, the other half would be seizing the opportunities still widely available in America and sharing in the wealth. There would be no such thing as a permanent "underclass." Ideally, every American would have access to the skills necessary to succeed and the knowledge necessary to be a good citizen.

To be a good citizen, I believe, you cannot fear contrary information. As we all learned in 2022, many of America's most influential people live in dread of learning something new. I watched in wonder at their panic when Elon Musk purchased Twitter and threw open its doors to a world of knowledge that had been locked away. On the subject of COVID-19 alone, the government–Big Tech collaboration screened out volumes of potentially lifesaving information. We are still assessing the damage.

Prior to his purchase of Twitter, the literal "African American" Musk—he was born in South Africa—had emerged as a modern-day Thomas Edison, a man who embodied both knowledge and progress. With his introduction of Tesla, a high-end electric vehicle, Musk had captured the imagination of the environmentally conscious. With his development of SpaceX, he appealed to adventurers and futurists. He was a man for all seasons and for all people. Save for those who hated billionaires in general, no major interest groups opposed him. "I'm nauseatingly pro-American," Musk has said. "I would have come here from any country. The U.S. is where great things are possible."[9]

Then, as it did with Booker T. Washington, politics muddied the waters. In opening up Twitter, Musk shed some necessary light on the ideologically driven censorship of the social media platforms. Despite his own political neutrality— Musk describes himself as a "moderate and a registered independent"—the media now attacked him for giving contrarians back their voice, especially conservative ones. A quick

Google search shows one negative headline after another, a relentless stream of them. This piling on reflects both the media's newfound disgust with Musk but also Google's use of algorithms to punish its enemies.

Many in the media, likely most, now hope for Musk to fail in all of his enterprises, even the ones in which they believe. This is a shame. Young people especially need role models that epitomize the power that knowledge holds. Charming and media-savvy, Musk is one such person. He has had the ability to make math and science "cool." His critics, however, could not abide a man who challenged their hold on knowledge. They had grown soft posting yard signs that read SCIENCE IS REAL, and shouting down anyone who would loosen their grip on the culture.

Dr. Ben Carson could have warned Musk what the future held for those who defied the orthodoxy of the day. If there were ever a good role model for a young man, particularly a disadvantaged young man of color, it was Dr. Carson. Born in 1951, Carson grew up in Detroit with a brother and a single mom under classically difficult circumstances. His family moved often. Carson attended inferior public schools in Detroit and a Seventh-day Adventist school in Boston that was even worse. "I was perhaps the worst student you have ever seen," said Carson. "You know, I thought I was stupid, all my classmates thought I was stupid, so there was general agreement."[10]

The one person who didn't think he was stupid was his mother. Despite her mental health issues, she pushed her sons to excel. She limited their time in front of a television set, kept them inside until they finished their homework, and insisted they read two books a week. The Carsons returned to Detroit, and the boys enjoyed the relative stability. At the predominantly Black Southwestern High School in Detroit, Carson found his calling in science and did well enough to earn a scholarship to Yale, from which he graduated with a degree in psychology. After Yale, he moved on to the University of Michigan Medical School.

If the "diversity" gods eased his path to Yale and perhaps even to Michigan, Carson turned his back on them the moment he shifted his focus to neurosurgery. This is a no-nonsense field that requires not only nimble fingers but also advanced powers of reasoning. Carson had found his gift and followed it to the renowned Johns Hopkins Hospital in Baltimore. Johns Hopkins designated Carson the director of pediatric neurosurgery when he was thirty-two, a position he would hold for nearly thirty years.

In 1987, at just thirty-five years of age, Carson made medical history and achieved national renown when he and his team of seventy support staff successfully separated a pair of Siamese twins who were joined at the brain. The twins survived, a feat that had never been done before. This was the first of his many scientific breakthroughs in the complex field of pediatric neurosurgery. Knowledge, says Carson in his advice to young people, "makes you into a more valuable person. The more knowledge you have, the more people need you. It's an interesting phenomenon, but when people need you, they pay you, so you'll be okay in life."[11]

Over the years, Carson was duly honored for his achievements. In 2001, the Library of Congress designated the fifty-year-old Carson a "Living Legend." In 2006, the NAACP awarded him its highest honor for outstanding achievement.

In 2008, the White House awarded Carson the Presidential Medal of Freedom. In 2015, Detroit Public Schools opened the Dr. Benjamin Carson High School of Science and Medicine, a fitting tribute to the one Detroit man who best exemplified science and medicine.

Even before the high school opened, however, Carson had quietly begun to ruffle feathers that were not supposed to be ruffled. In 2013, with President Barack Obama and First Lady Michelle Obama in attendance, Carson gave the keynote speech at the National Prayer Breakfast. The proudly Christian doctor began by citing Proverbs 11:9, "'With his mouth the godless destroys his neighbor, but through knowledge the righteous escapes.'" For Carson, knowledge opened doors, but political correctness closed them.[12]

"But PC is dangerous," said Carson to an audience, the president included, that was not expecting to hear this message. "Because, you see, [in] this country one of the founding principles was freedom of thought and freedom of expression, and it muffles people. It puts a muzzle on them." Du Bois had said much the same thing a century earlier, but at that time progressives agreed with him on the value of free speech. A century later, their woke heirs fear freedom of expression the way Dracula feared the dawn.

The nation, Carson continued, was also founded on the idea that its citizens would be literate. "The people who founded this nation said that our system of government was designed for a well-informed and educated populace, and when they become less informed, they become vulnerable." Here he echoes Booker T. Washington. This is why, said Carson, education is essential to the life of a nation, so essential that he and his wife,

Candy, started a Carson Scholarship program designed to elevate the status of learning, particularly in inner-city schools. Knowledge was critical, Carson continued, if the nation was to solve the problems it faced. He then identified a series of problems from the deficit to health care and proposed solutions that did not please insiders of either political party.

Like Washington and Du Bois before him, Carson felt the need to share his insights with the nation at large. So on May 4, 2015, he took the stage in Detroit and announced his candidacy for president. By his side was Candy, his wife of forty years. Sitting in the front row were his three sons—one an engineer, one an entrepreneur, one a CPA, all three with their wives. Carson spoke warmly of his sons' grandmother, a woman with a third-grade education and a stubborn belief that "America remains a place of dreams," a vision her sons and grandsons more than fulfilled.[13]

The soft-spoken Carson focused on the role education played in his life. Under pressure from his mother to read, Carson was intrigued by "people of accomplishment." In tracking their life stories, he said, "I began to recognize that the person who has the most to do with what happens to you in life is you." He identified with people throughout American history who "knew how to do things" and did them. Fundamental to their success and the success of the nation was the recognition by our founders that "our freedom and our way of life is dependent on a well-informed and educated populace." Knowledge not only empowered the individual, but it also strengthened the nation.

For a political outsider, Carson did well in a crowded primary field. His strong beliefs and conciliatory style resonated.

From among the seventeen Republican candidates, he was one of the last few standing. Offered a position in President Trump's cabinet as Secretary of Housing and Urban Development, he accepted. This affiliation gave the "politically correct" activists that Carson warned about in his presidential announcement speech all the excuse they needed to attack Carson in his own hometown.

Like Clarence Thomas, Carson was not seen as a community kind of guy. Thus, in November 2022, a week after the GOP won back the House, the Detroit school board voted to rename the Dr. Benjamin Carson High School of Science and Medicine. "There was no debate about the name change," a local publication reported. Carson's alleged sin was to have "courted controversy during his tenure as housing secretary in the Trump administration." The school was renamed for a woman, the late Dr. Ethelene Crockett, a leftist champion of abortion and the first Black American woman in Michigan to become board certified in obstetrics and gynecology.[14]

Some fifty-five of his former staffers at HUD signed a letter in protest of the name change. "The truth is, Dr. Carson should have dozens of schools named after him," said the letter. "We firmly believe removing the name of a man like this leaves us all the worse off for it, especially the students this political stunt purports to set an example for. We hope each student aspires to be the type of leader Dr. Carson is: a compassionate and humble man that cares deeply about the future of our children."[15]

The fifth man of knowledge to be discussed has been a role model for me, especially in my understanding of the way economies work. He has been a role model, too, in his willingness to ignore the unwritten guidelines on how an intellectual is supposed to think, especially a Black intellectual. Jason Riley titled his book on economist Thomas Sowell *Maverick* for good reason.

Born in 1930 in Jim Crow North Carolina into a home without electricity or hot running water, Sowell was an orphan by the age of three. He was raised by a great-aunt as one of her own and moved with her to Harlem when he was eight. For all the talk of systemic racism, New York was not North Carolina. As a freshman, Sowell was offered a spot at New York City's highly selective Stuyvesant High School, a school that students have to test their way into. Today, many consider color-blind testing racist if the results displease them. When Sowell took the test, such testing was seen as a sign of progress. For reasons that Sowell has not been shy to explain, Black students did relatively better in the 1940s, when he applied, than they do today.

Labeled a "wayward youth" by the juvenile courts, Sowell dropped out of Stuyvesant at sixteen and for the next ten or so years got all of his education from what he calls "the school of hard knocks." He worked a series of odd jobs, served in the U.S. Marines, and gained "a lasting respect for the common sense of ordinary people."[16] Sowell did not graduate from college until his late twenties, then went on to graduate school at Columbia University and the University of Chicago, where he studied under one of my other sources of inspiration, Milton Friedman.

It is Sowell's combination of intellectual insight and common sense that has made him such a popular author. Although he tackles complex subjects, Sowell has chosen to write his forty-five or so books in "plainspoken prose."[17] As a result, many of his books have become bestsellers.

One chapter of the book *Maverick* is titled "Sowell Man," an obvious pun but also a serious inquiry into the virtues needed to be a knowledgeable *man*, especially in a society that does not value real knowledge. The chapter recounts an interview Sowell had with C-SPAN's generally fair Brian Lamb. Lamb asked how Sowell dealt with those "people of your own race" who think of him as a race traitor. An opponent of affirmative action, Sowell had often run afoul of those "organized noisemakers" who claim to be spokespeople for their race. As he told Lamb, if controversial viewpoints are to be advanced, someone has to advance them.[18]

Throughout his long and storied career, Sowell has shown an impressive indifference to those noisemakers. To be a knowledgeable man requires much more than an education. It requires a willingness to meld that education with real lived experience and to defend truths no matter how unpopular. As Riley observes, for decades now "liberal elites [have] placed the onus on whites to fix the problems of blacks." Sowell won't have that. Maverick that he is, he has ignored the intellectuals of all races who clamor for a collective response to society's problems. Sowell believes in the individual. He believes in agency. He celebrates "people who are seeking alternatives, people who have challenged the conventional wisdom on one or more issues, people who have thought for themselves instead of marching in step and chanting familiar refrains."[19]

The American Man

In the course of researching and writing this book, I have had to confront the chaos of contemporary culture and reexamine my own self-professed libertarianism. Says Mark Levin, "There is a fine line between libertarianism and anarchy." A young man can afford to walk that line. Perhaps a father cannot.

This does not mean conforming to a morally disordered culture. As Thomas Sowell reminds us, to be a man today, you have to be a maverick. You have to resist the siren call of the elites who want you to march in step, who want you to remain dependent, unquestioning, ignorant. To assert your dignity as a protector, as a provider, as a father, as a husband, as a man of

God, is to challenge the powers that be, even risk your career. As easy as it is to despair, it is much more productive to stand up and speak your piece. A good place to begin is by evaluating your own role in the world. Through my conversations and my research, I have discovered a lot about my own values and what it takes to be a man in today's society.

I continue to believe that Jesus is still the way. For years, I have been disgruntled with the Church and with good reason. But the preacher's kid in me is alive and well even when I try to deny it. The prodigal son always comes back home, however grudgingly.

I have a deep respect for tradition, and I always have. Norms and institutions were created for a reason. The more I learn, the deeper is that respect.

The people who navigated this experiment called life have too much knowledge and wisdom to ignore. Our elders' leadership is essential. We are fools to turn our backs on it.

I continue to believe people should be allowed to make their own decisions as long as we don't inflict pain on others.

Some things are just true and our inability to say what is true has damaged us as a society. Many of us have meant well when we accept behaviors believing that to each his own. But sometimes when you give folks an inch, they will take your culture and trash it. It is time to evaluate every inch we give.

Men are men. Women are women. There are only two sexes. We still can love our brothers and sisters who believe otherwise, but we do society a disservice by pretending they are right.

As men, we must lead our homes and love our women as Christ loved the Church. And just as Christ loved the Church, we must show our love for our women even when our ego is challenged in so doing. We must be willing to do the work to create harmony in our homes and by extension in society.

I have learned that my dad wasn't that different from the dads of the men for whom I have the deepest respect. Like them, he may have tailored his lessons for his two headstrong Black sons of Texas, but he pulled his lessons from the wisdom of the ages. It is that greater wisdom that holds us together as a culture and as a nation. As men it is our duty to pass it along.

Finally, little has changed since Adam. Our ego and pride continue to be our downfall. I will be the first to admit these are failings of my own, but trust me—I'm working on them!

Acknowledgments

Thanks to:

The American Men, Ben Watson, Sean Hannity, Mark Levin, Devon Still, Dean Cain, Pete Hegseth, and Dr. Tony Evans.

Neurophysiologist Dr. Lauren Miller.

Fox News Management Team.

Suzanne Scott, Meade Cooper, Lauren Petterson, Megan Albano, and Gavin Hadden.

Fox News Producers: Hayley, Tim, Alex, Scott, and Shannon.

Notes

Introduction: The War on Masculinity

1. "The Fridging Dead: The Walking Dead's Patriarchal Problem," *The Artifice*, December 5, 2014, https://the-artifice.com/the-walking-dead-patriarchal-problem/.
2. "APA Guidelines for Psychological Practice with Boys and Men," August 2018, https://www.apa.org/about/policy/boys-men-practice-guidelines.pdf.
3. Conservative Momma, Twitter, January 1, 2023, https://twitter.com/conmomma/status/1609727501017944066.
4. Interview with Pastor Tony Evans, February 7, 2023. Unless otherwise cited, all subsequent references to Evans come from this interview.
5. Brett Schenker, "Facebook Demographics: The Walking Dead, Not All Media Are Created Equal," Comics Beat, October 31, 2013, https://www.comicsbeat.com/facebook-demographics-the-walking-dead-not-all-media-are-created-equal/#:~:text=Walking%20Dead%20fans%20are%2059.38,when%20it%20comes%20to%20that.
6. Interview with Dean Cain, February 24, 2023. All subsequent references to Cain come from this interview.
7. Aaron Sibarium, "'Absolutely Insane': Connecticut Law Would Axe Fitness Requirements for Female Firefighters," *Washington Free Beacon*, January 18, 2023, https://freebeacon.com/latest-news/absolutely-insane-connecticut-law-would-axe-fitness-requirements-for-female-firefighters/.
8. Toni Airaksinen, "College's 'Deconstruct Masculinity' Program Doubles in Size," *Campus Reform*, October 27, 2017, https://www.campusreform.org/article?id=10051.

9. Toni Airaksinen, "UConn to Help Men Stop 'Mansplaining,' 'Interrupting Others,'" *Campus Reform*, November 10, 2017, https://www.campusreform.org/article?id=10130.
10. Sandor Farkas, "College Program Will Help Students Cope with 'Toxic Masculinity,'" *Campus Reform*, September 19, 2017, https://www.campusreform.org/article?id=9801.
11. Alia Dastagir, "Marsha Blackburn Asked Ketanji Brown Jackson to Define 'Woman.' Science Says There's No Simple Answer," *USA Today*, March 24, 2022, https://www.usatoday.com/story/life/health-wellness/2022/03/24/marsha-blackburn-asked-ketanji-jackson-define-woman-science/7152439001/.
12. Interview with Mark Levin, February 17, 2023. Unless otherwise cited, all subsequent references to Levin come from this interview.

Chapter 1: Man as Father

1. Luke Russert, "Preface," in Tim Russert, *Big Russ and Me: Father and Son: Lessons of Life*, Kindle edition (New York: Weinstein Books, 2014), location 117. The Preface will be cited by location.
2. Tim Russert, 23.
3. Evans interview.
4. Tim Russert, 18.
5. Luke Russert, location 284.
6. Tim Russert, 24.
7. Luke Russert, location 187.
8. Tim Russert, 31.
9. Ibid., 43.
10. Ibid.
11. Ibid., 220.
12. Ibid., 218.
13. Shaye Galletta, "Why Do Professional Athletes Go Broke?" Fox Business, February 2, 2022, https://www.foxbusiness.com/personal-finance/why-do-professional-athletes-go-broke.
14. Russert, 227.
15. Ibid., 228.
16. Ibid., 302.
17. Luke Russert, location 96.
18. Pope John Paul II, *Evangelium Vitae*, https://www.vatican.va/content/john-paul-ii/en/encyclicals/documents/hf_jp-ii_enc_25031995_evangelium-vitae.html.
19. Evans interview.
20. Mario Cuomo, "Religious Belief and Public Morality: A Catholic

Governor's Perspective," University of Notre Dame Archives, http://archives.nd.edu/research/texts/cuomo.htm.

21. Pope John Paul II, *Evangelium Vitae*, https://www.vatican.va/content /john-paul-ii/en/encyclicals/documents/hf_jp-ii_enc_25031995 _evangelium-vitae.html.

22. Frederick Douglass, *Narrative of the Life of Frederick Douglass*, first published in 1845, Kindle edition (Red Skull Publishing, 2015), location 172.

23. "Lawrence Jones' Mother Knew She Had Responsibility upon Pregnancy," Fox News, May 16, 2022, https://www.youtube.com /watch?v=FCXzDQ3w0Nk.

24. "Obama's Father's Day Remarks," Transcript, *New York Times*, June 15, 2008, https://www.nytimes.com/2008/06/15/us/politics /15text-obama.html.

25. Interview with Jack Brewer, February 13, 2023.

26. "Distribution of Child Population in the United States in 2021, by Family Structure and Race," Statista, https://www.statista.com /statistics/458071/percentage-of-children-in-the-us-by-family -structure-and-race/.

27. Thomas Edsall, "'It's Become Increasingly Hard for Them to Feel Good About Themselves,'" *New York Times*, September 22, 2021, https://www.nytimes.com/2021/09/22/opinion/economy-education -women-men.html.

28. Naomi Schaefer Riley, "Women Who Let Boyfriends Abuse Their Kids Must Pay the Price," *New York Post*, August 20, 2022, https://nypost.com/2022/08/20/women-who-let-boyfriends-abuse -their-kids-must-pay-the-price/.

29. Brown v. Quayle, *Baltimore Sun*, May 21, 1992, https://www .baltimoresun.com/news/bs-xpm-1992-05-22-1992143210 -story.html.

30. "How the Original 'Murphy Brown' Caused Controversy," *Time*, September 27, 2018, https://time.com/5405100/murphy-brown -cultural-importance-reboot/.

31. Ibid.

32. Diana Clark, "We Know What Makes a Man. But What Makes a Woman?" *Evie*, August 2, 2012, https://www.eviemagazine.com /post/we-know-what-makes-a-man-but-what-makes-a-woman.

33. Evans interview.

34. Barbara Dafoe Whitehead, "Dan Quayle Was Right," *The Atlantic*, April 1, 1993, https://www.theatlantic.com/magazine/archive /1993/04/dan-quayle-was-right/307015/.

35. Interview with Dr. Lauren Miller, February 17, 2023. All subsequent references to Miller come from this interview.
36. Gary Susman, "Candice Bergen Says Dan Quayle Was Right," *EW*, July 11, 2002, https://ew.com/article/2002/07/11/candice-bergen-says-dan-quayle-was-right/.
37. Cassie Jaye, "Meeting the Enemy," TED Talk, October 18, 2017, https://www.youtube.com/watch?v=3WMuzhQXJoY.
38. Snejana Farberov, "Texas Dad Fears Ex-Wife Plans to 'Chemically Castrate' 9-Year-Old Son," *New York Post*, January 6, 2023, https://nypost.com/2023/01/06/texas-dad-fears-ex-wife-plans-to-chemically-castrate-9-year-old-son/.
39. Larry and Andy Wachowski, *The Matrix*, https://www.dailyscript.com/scripts/the_matrix.pdf.
40. Charles Blow, "Fathers' Sons and Brothers' Keepers," *New York Times*, February 28, 2014, https://www.nytimes.com/2014/03/01/opinion/blow-fathers-sons-and-brothers-keepers.html.
41. Interview with Pete Hegseth, February 26, 2023. All subsequent references to Hegseth come from this interview.
42. Evans interview.
43. Matthew 19:6.
44. Evans interview.

Chapter 2: Man as Protector

1. Jessica Schladebeck, "Off-Duty Border Patrol Agent Borrowed Barber's Gun, Rushed to Texas School After Wife Texted 'Help,'" *New York Daily News*, May 27, 2022, https://www.police1.com/police-heroes/articles/off-duty-border-patrol-agent-borrowed-barbers-gun-rushed-to-texas-school-after-wife-texted-help-cjI75IWJtBjYN8ct/.
2. Michael Cantu, "Central Texas Father Stands Guard Outside School: 'I Could Not Sleep After Uvalde,'" KBTX, May 26, 2022, https://www.kbtx.com/2022/05/26/central-texas-father-stands-guard-outside-school-i-could-not-sleep-after-uvalde/.
3. Steffi Cao, "The Uvalde Mom Who Ran into the School to Save Her Sons from the Shooting Spoke Out About How Police Tried to Stop Her," BuzzFeed News, June 4, 2022, https://www.buzzfeednews.com/article/stefficao/uvalde-mom-saved-sons-school-shooting-police.
4. "Texas Father Jumps Out of His Seat to Save His Bull Riding Son," ABC 13 Houston, May 2, 2022, https://www.youtube.com/watch?v=0mJBQpbWiYA.

5. Ramsey Solutions, "The 7 Baby Steps," https://www.ramseysolutions
    .com/dave-ramsey-7-baby-steps.
6. "Denzel Washington Blames Black Crime on Lack of Father
    Figures," RegalMag.com, https://www.regalmag.com/archives
    /additional-archives/denzel-washington-blames-black-crime
    -on-lack-of-father-figures/.
7. *The Odyssey of Homer*, translated by Samuel Butler, revised by
    Timothy Power and Gregory Nagy, https://cyber.harvard.edu
    /homer/odyssey.html.
8. Rachael Pace, "20 Signs a Guy Is Protective of You," Marriage.com,
    May 16, 2022, https://www.marriage.com/advice/relationship
    /signs-a-guy-is-protective-of-you/.
9. Alexis de Tocqueville, *Democracy in America*, Book I, Chapter 14,
    https://xroads.virginia.edu/~Hyper/DETOC/1_ch14.htm.
10. Ibid., Book II, Chapter 9.
11. Veronica Neffinger, "Former NFL Quarterback Kurt Warner Thanks
    Jesus in Hall of Fame Speech," Christian Headlines, August 10, 2017,
    https://www.christianheadlines.com/blog/former-nfl-quarterback
    -kurt-warner-thanks-jesus-in-speech.html.
12. Ron Howard and Clint Howard, *The Boys: A Memoir of Hollywood
    and Family*, Nook edition (New York: William Morrow, 2021).
13. Evans interview.
14. Howard and Howard, 109.
15. "Macaulay Culkin Takes Another Role," ABC News, January 6,
    2020, https://abcnews.go.com/2020/story?id=124083&page
    =1#:~:text=But%20now%2C%20at%20the%20age,life%20from
    %20an%20older%20woman.
16. Bernard Weinraub, "The Talk of Hollywood: It Seems the Father of
    the Child Star Is the Enfant Terrible," *New York Times*, November 1,
    1993, https://www.nytimes.com/1993/11/01/movies/talk-hollywood
    -it-seems-father-child-star-enfant-terrible.html.
17. Katie Nicholl, "No Woman Can Be Hit Like This and Stay with Her
    Man," *Daily Mail*, August 6, 2016, https://www.dailymail.co.uk
    /tvshowbiz/article-3727329/No-woman-hit-like-stay-man
    -Dramatic-exclusive-pictures-violent-scuffle-terrified-Lindsay
    -Lohan-playboy-ex-Mykonos-beach-troubled-lister-reveals
    -relationship-over.html.
18. Katherine Webb, "All the Child Stars Who Sued Their Parents,"
    Show Biz Cheat Sheet, June 6, 2018, https://www.cheatsheet.com
    /entertainment/child-stars-who-sued-their-parents.html/.
19. Howard and Howard, 109.

20. Ibid.
21. Interview with Ben Watson, February 7, 2023. All subsequent references to Watson come from this interview.
22. Interview with Sean Hannity, February 17, 2023. All subsequent references to Hannity come from this interview.

Chapter 3: The Godly Man

1. "Understanding Historical Actors," Lumen Learning, https:// courses.lumenlearning.com/wm-ushistory1/chapter/historical-hack -understanding-historical-actors/.
2. Jon Ackerman, "Bills QB Josh Allen Describes His 'Spiritual Awakening' in Events Surrounding Damar Hamlin," Sports Spectrum, January 13, 2023, https://sportsspectrum.com/sport /football/2023/01/13/bills-qb-josh-allen-spiritual-awakening-damar -hamlin/.
3. Tony Evans, "Kingdom Voting Series: God and Freedom," September 20, 2020, Facebook, https://www.facebook.com /drtonyevans/videos/723141354937029/.
4. Tony Evans, *Kingdom Marriage: Connecting God's Purpose with Your Pleasure*, Kindle edition (Carol Stream, Illinois: Tyndale House Publishers, 2016), 66.
5. Abraham Lincoln: Timeline, https://www.workoutyourfaith.com /timeline/lincoln.
6. Ibid.
7. Ibid.
8. Abraham Lincoln, Second Inaugural Address, March 4, 1865, National Park Service, https://www.nps.gov/linc/learn /historyculture/lincoln-second-inaugural.htm.
9. Evans, "Kingdom Voting Series."
10. Josef Stalin, "Stalin's Address to the People," May 9, 1945, https:// www.marxists.org/reference/archive/stalin/works/1945/05 /09a.htm.
11. William Wilberforce Quotes, https://quotefancy.com /william-wilberforce-quotes.
12. "William Lloyd Garrison Introduces *The Liberator*," 1831, https://www.americanyawp.com/reader/religion-and-reform /william-lloyd-garrison-introduces-the-liberator-1831/.
13. William Lloyd Garrison, from the Introduction to Frederick Douglass, *Narrative of the Life of Frederick Douglass*, first published in 1845, Kindle edition (Red Skull Publishing, 2015), location 66.
14. Frederick Douglass, *The Collected Works*, Kindle edition (Colorado Springs: Musaicum Books, 2018), location 3323.

15. Thomas Jefferson, *Notes on the State of Virginia*, Electronic edition, Documenting the American South, https://docsouth.unc.edu /southlit/jefferson/jefferson.html.
16. Douglass, *Narrative*, 597.
17. Ibid., 633.
18. Ibid.
19. Ibid., 727.
20. Ibid., 714.
21. Ibid., 465.
22. Ibid., 876.
23. Ibid., 999.
24. Douglass, *Collected Works*, location 1479.
25. Evans, *Kingdom Marriage*, 66.
26. Douglass, *Collected Works*, location 872.
27. Ibid., 874.
28. "William Lloyd Garrison, 1805–1879: The Story of His Life Told by His Children," Internet Archive, https://archive.org/stream /williamlloydgarr04garr/williamlloydgarr04garr_djvu.txt.
29. William Lloyd Garrison, "Valedictory: The Last Number of *The Liberator*," http://fair-use.org/the-liberator/1865/12/29/valedictory.
30. Mary Eberstadt, "Regular Christians Are No Longer Welcome in American Culture," *Time*, June 29, 2016, https://time.com/4385755 /faith-in-america/.
31. Meeke Addison, "The Stated Goals of Black Lives Matter Are Anti-Christian," *Decision*, July 1, 2020, https://decisionmagazine .com/the-stated-goals-of-black-lives-matter-are-anti-christian/.
32. Martin Luther King Jr., "Letter from Birmingham Jail," May 19, 1963, Jack Miller Center, https://jackmillercenter.org/martin-luther -kings-letter-birmingham-jail/.
33. Evans, "Kingdom Voting Series."

Chapter 4: The Disciplined Man

1. Gehan Roberts, "Nature and Nurture: Why Do Boys and Girls Behave Differently?" *The Conversation*, March 4, 2012, https:// theconversation.com/nature-and-nurture-why-do-boys-and-girls -behave-differently-2920.
2. Adam Teicher, "Success, Trust and Burnt Ends: Why Everyone Loves Kansas City Chiefs Coach Andy Reid," ESPN, January 31, 2021, https://www.espn.com/nfl/story/_/id/30424487/why-everyone -loves-chiefs-coach-andy-reid.
3. "Tyreek Hill Bio: Early Life, Career, Net Worth & Legal Cases," PlayersBio, January 1, 2023, https://playersbio.com/tyreek-hill/.

4. Tadd Haislop, "Tyreek Hill's Timeline of Trouble: From a Domestic Violence Arrest in College to Child Abuse Investigation with Chiefs," *Sporting News*, February 2, 2020, https://www.sportingnews.com/us/nfl/news/tyreek-hill-domestic-violence-child-abuse-investigation/neqfn40200lt16ik2142ay772.
5. Kevin Van Valkenburg, "A Week in the Life of a Coach," ESPN, November 22, 2013, https://www.espn.com/nfl/story/_/id/10012376/baltimore-ravens-head-coach-john-harbaugh-clocks-long-hours-prep-game-day-espn-magazine.
6. Joe Drape, "What Any Parent Would Do," *New York Times*, November 3, 2022, https://www.nytimes.com/2022/11/01/sports/football/britt-reid-sentence-andy.html.
7. Clarence Thomas, *My Grandfather's Son: A Memoir*, Kindle edition (New York: Harper Collins, 2007), 2.
8. Ibid., 6.
9. Ibid., 12.
10. Ibid.
11. Ibid., 15.
12. Andrea Sedlak et al., "Fourth National Incidence Study of Child Abuse and Neglect," 2010, https://www.childhelp.org/wp-content/uploads/2015/07/Sedlak-A.-J.-et-al.-2010-Fourth-National-Incidence-Study-of-Child-Abuse-and-Neglect-NIS%E2%80%934.pdf.
13. Thomas, 25.
14. Ibid., 68.
15. Ibid., 25.
16. Ibid., 26.
17. Ibid., 17.
18. Ibid., 52.
19. Ibid., 73.
20. Ibid., 184.
21. Ibid.
22. *Roe v. Wade*, 410 U.S. 113, Decided January 22, 1973, https://supreme.justia.com/cases/federal/us/410/113/#tab-opinion-1950136.
23. Thomas, 184.
24. Ibid., 260.
25. "Clarence Thomas Responds to Anita Hill," YouTube, https://www.youtube.com/watch?v=ZURHD5BU1o8.
26. Thomas, 169.

Chapter 5: The Chivalrous Man

1. Henry Atkins, "10 Facts About Medieval Knights and Chivalry," *History Hit*, June 19, 2018, https://www.historyhit.com/facts-about -medieval-knights-and-chivalry/.
2. Cynthia Wachtell, "The Author of the Civil War," *New York Times*, July 6, 2012, https://archive.nytimes.com/opinionator.blogs.nytimes .com/2012/07/06/the-author-of-the-civil-war/.
3. Annika Jensen, "Finally Speaking Up: Sexual Assault in the Civil War Era," The Gettysburg Compiler, October 5, 2015, https:// gettysburgcompiler.org/2015/10/05/finally-speaking-up-sexual -assault-in-the-civil-war-era/.
4. "Titanic Disaster: Official Casualty Figures," ANESI.com, https:// www.anesi.com/titanic.htm#:~:text=%22More%20men %20survived%20than%20women,to%2074.35%25%20of%20the %20women.
5. Thomas Maugh, "Women and Children First, Maybe," *Los Angeles Times*, May 2, 2010, https://www.latimes.com/archives/la-xpm -2010-mar-02-la-sci-titanic-web2-2010mar02-story.html.
6. Lyman Stone, "Male Sexlessness Is Rising but Not for the Reasons Incels Claim," Institute for Family Studies, May 14, 2018, https:// ifstudies.org/blog/male-sexlessness-is-rising-but-not-for-the -reasons-incels-claim.
7. Josh Hawley, "Senator Josh Hawley Shreds Everything About the Left," YouTube, https://www.youtube.com/watch?v=zz5HsVpI-iA.
8. All comments follow Hawley clip on Twitter, https://twitter.com /Acyn/status/1604625823419359232.
9. "Man Saves Woman from Burning Car," KCRA, March 6, 2022, https://www.youtube.com/watch?v=pUa83YMhnz.
10. "Mystery Man Saves Woman from Drowning in Rip Current at St. Augustine Beach," First Coast News, May 26, 2020, https://www .youtube.com/watch?v=8pnU-3nW0jU.
11. "Diocese of Brooklyn Honors Good Samaritan Who Helped Save Stranger in Union Square Subway Attack," CBS News, July 20, 2021, https://www.cbsnews.com/newyork/news/sean-conaboy -diocese-of-brooklyn-medal-union-square-subway-stabbing/.
12. Alex Rose, "Philly Man Sentenced in Sex Assault at 69th Street Terminal," *Delco Times*, December 26, 2022, https://www .delcotimes.com/2022/12/28/philly-man-gets-county-sentence -in-attempted-indecent-assault/.
13. "Fiston Ngoy, Charged in Rape on SEPTA Train, Held for Trial," CBS Philadelphia, November 29, 2021, https://www.cbsnews.com

/philadelphia/news/fiston-ngoy-charged-septa-rape-train-held
-trial/.

14 Baldwin Arts and Academics Magnet School Summer Suggested
Reading List 2019, https://piperlibraryfiles.com/CKFinder
/connector?command=Proxy&type=Montgomery&currentFolder=
/&fileName=Baldwin+Arts+and+Academics+Magnet.pdf&cache
=31536000.

15. "20 Contemporary Books for Your High School Reading List,"
Prestwick House, April 20, 2019, https://www.prestwickhouse.com
/blog/post/2019/04/20-contemporary-books-for-your-high-school
-reading-list.

16. Cormac McCarthy, *The Road* (New York: Alfred A. Knopf, 2006), 4.

17. Jane McFann, "Boys and Books," Reading Rockets, https://www
.readingrockets.org/article/boys-and-books.

18. "Disney Aims to Empower New Generation of Girls in Promising
New Shows," NCTA, March 4, 2022, https://www.ncta.com/whats
-new/disney-aims-empower-new-generation-of-girls-in-promising
-new-shows.

19. Matthew Stewart and Paul Sheehan, "Top 10 Disney Heroines
Ranked," Gold Derby, https://www.goldderby.com/gallery/best
-disney-heroines-ranked/heroines-elsa/.

20. Britt Hennemuth, "Rachel Zegler on Snow White, Spielberg, and
the Time Lady Gaga Fixed Her Wardrobe Malfunction," *Vanity
Fair*, October 14, 2022, https://www.vanityfair.com/hollywood
/2022/10/rachel-zegler-on-snow-white-spielberg-lady-gaga.

21. Alyssa Meyers and Sarah Shevenock, "Is Gen Z Too Cool for
Marvel? Just 9% of Marvel Fans Identify as Part of the Generation,"
Morning Consult, December 6, 2021, https://morningconsult.com
/2021/12/06/is-gen-z-too-cool-for-marvel/.

22. R. J. Shaw, "The Feminization of Your Heroes, Your Stories & You,"
YouTube, March 26, 2022, https://www.youtube.com/watch?v
=FwX3GLm73IE.

23. Angelique Nairn, "For the Love of Thor! Why It's So Hard for
Marvel to Get Its Female Superheroes Right," *The Conversation*,
July 11, 2022, https://theconversation.com/for-the-love-of-thor
-why-its-so-hard-for-marvel-to-get-its-female-superheroes-right
-186639.

24. "Good Books for Boys Written by Men," Listopia, https://www
.goodreads.com/list/show/38524.Good_Books_for_Boys_Written
_by_Men.

25. Craig Elvy, "Galadriel in The Rings of Power Is Very Different
to LOTR's Portrayal," Screen Rant, October 12, 2022, https://

screenrant.com/lotr-rings-power-galadriel-shows-movies
-comparison-different/.

Chapter 6: The Timely Man

1. "Benjamin Franklin Quotes About Time," AZ Quotes, https://bit
   .ly/3Paoc0N.
2. Benjamin Franklin, Project Gutenberg's Autobiography of Benjamin
   Franklin, Chapter IX, https://www.gutenberg.org/files/20203
   /20203-h/20203-h.htm.
3. "Surprising Railroad Inventions: U.S. Time Zones," Union Pacific,
   https://www.up.com/customers/track-record/tr031020-time-zones
   .htm#:~:text=On%20November%2018,%201883,%20the,are
   %20still%20in%20place%20today.
4. *Crash*, screenplay by Paul Haggis and Bobby Moresco, https://assets
   .scriptslug.com/live/pdf/scripts/crash-2004.pdf.
5. William Shakespeare, *The Merry Wives of Windsor*, Act 2, Scene 2.
6. Jack London quotes, Goodreads, https://www.goodreads.com
   /quotes/346314-the-proper-function-of-man-is-to-live-not-to.

Chapter 7: The Resilient Man

1. Theodore Roosevelt, "Citizenship in a Republic," May 5, 1910,
   Theodore Roosevelt Center, https://www.theodorerooseveltcenter
   .org/Learn-About-TR/TR-Encyclopedia/Culture-and-Society
   /Man-in-the-Arena.aspx.
2. Theodore Roosevelt, *Ranch Life and the Hunting-Trail* (New York:
   Century Company, 1888), 56.
3. "Muhammad Ali: 9 Famous Quotes from the Boxing Legend," *The
   Hollywood Reporter*, June 3, 2016, https://www.hollywoodreporter
   .com/news/general-news/muhammad-ali-quotes-famous-lines
   -899565/.
4. George W. Ball, "The Lessons of Vietnam," *New York Times*, April 1,
   1973, https://www.nytimes.com/1973/04/01/archives/have-we
   -learned-or-only-failed-the-lessons-of-vietnam-vietnam.html.
5. Jim Valvano, "Don't Give Up," March 3, 1993, https://jamesclear
   .com/great-speeches/dont-give-up-by-jim-valvano.
6. Mark Abadi, "Eagles Quarterback Nick Foles' Super Bowl Victory
   Speech Has an Important Lesson About Failure," *Business Insider*,
   January 11, 2019, https://www.businessinsider.com/nick-foles
   -super-bowl-speech-failure-2018-2#:~:text=%22Failure%20is%20a
   %20part%20of,thousands%20of%20times,%20made%20mistakes.
7. Marc Fisher, "Jackie's 50th," *Washington Post*, April 16, 1997, https://

www.washingtonpost.com/archive/politics/1997/04/16
/jackies-50th/2f5b7e61-a21d-4cec-984a-3ed896c020bb/.

8. Devika Pawar, "Tiger Woods Pays Tribute to Lee Elder: 'To Be Able
to Fight for Something You Believe in. I Don't Think He Gets Enough
Credit for That,'" Essentially Sports, December 2, 2021, https://www
.essentiallysports.com/golf-news-tiger-woods-pays-tribute-to-lee
-elder-to-be-able-to-fight-for-something-you-believe-in-i-dont-think
-he-gets-enough-credit-for-that/.

9. Michael Fletcher, "Tiger Woods Says He's 'Cablinasian,' but the
Police Only Saw Black," Andscape, May 30, 2017, https://andscape
.com/features/tiger-woods-dui-arrest-police-only-saw-black/.

10. "After Spine Surgery, Tiger Woods Wins the 2019 Masters," Advent
Health, April 15, 2019, https://www.adventhealth.com/blog/after
-spine-surgery-tiger-woods-wins-2019-masters.

11. "What Tiger Said in His Masters Winner's Press Conference," Golf
Channel, April 14, 2019, https://www.golfchannel.com/news/what
-tiger-woods-said-his-2019-masters-winners-press-conference.

12. David McCullough, *The Wright Brothers*, Kindle edition (New York:
Simon & Schuster, 2015), 39.

13. Ibid., 51.

14. Ibid., 52.

15. Ibid., 65.

16. Ibid., 82.

17. Ibid.

18. Ibid., 97.

19. Ibid., 111.

20. Ibid., 160.

21. Ibid., 209.

22. Ibid., 104.

23. Ibid., 236.

24. Brent Schlender and Rick Tetzeli, *Becoming Steve Jobs: The Evolution
of a Reckless Upstart into a Visionary Leader*, Kindle edition (New
York: Crown, 2015), 42.

25. Ibid.

26. Ibid., 43.

27. Ibid., 84.

28. Ibid., 85.

29. Ibid.

30. Ibid.

31. Ibid.

32. Ibid., 98.

33. Ibid., 119.

34. Ibid., 136.
35. Ibid.
36. Ibid., 137.
37. Ibid., 194.
38. Ibid., 147.
39. Ibid., 191.
40. Ibid., 31.
41. Jake Simpson, "O'Keefe Story Compared to Watergate, Civil Rights, Disco," *The Atlantic*, February 2, 2010, https://www.theatlantic.com/politics/archive/2010/02/o-keefe-story-compared-to-watergate-civil-rights-disco/346783/.
42. James O'Keefe, *Breakthrough: Our Guerrilla War to Expose Fraud and Save Democracy* (New York: Simon & Schuster, 2013), 156.
43. Ibid., 158.
44. "Enroll America Employee Resigns Following Project Veritas Investigation," Project Veritas, November 26, 2013, https://www.projectveritas.com/video/enroll-america-employee-resigns-following-project-veritas-investigation/.
45. Tom Scheck, "Words and Deeds out of Alignment for Potential Cabinet Appointment and Fox News Personality," March 27, 2018, https://www.apmreports.org/story/2018/03/27/pete-hegseth-potential-cabinet-appointment.

Chapter 8: The Fit Man

1. "The End of Men," A Tucker Carlson Original, Fox Nation, October 5, 2022, https://nation.foxnews.com/tucker-carlson-originals/.
2. Rick Reilly, "Life of Reilly," ESPN, April 14, 2009, https://www.espn.com/espnmag/story?id=4068270.
3. "Obesity, Race/Ethnicity, and COVID-19," Centers for Disease Control and Prevention, https://www.cdc.gov/obesity/data/obesity-and-covid-19.html.
4. Jagdish Khubchandani et al., "COVID-19 Pandemic and Weight Gain in American Adults: A Nationwide Population-Based Study," PubMed Central, January 16, 2022, https://www.ncbi.nlm.nih.gov/pmc/articles/PMC8743853/.
5. Laura Hillenbrand, *Unbroken: A World War II Story of Survival, Resilience, and Redemption* (New York: Random House, 2010), 155.
6. Hillenbrand, 189.
7. "'Unbroken's' Louis Zamperini: The Rest of the Story," CBN, https://www1.cbn.com/content/unbrokens-louis-zamperini-rest-story.
8. Hillenbrand, 386.

9. Nell Minow, "Unbroken: Path to Redemption," RogerEbert.com, September 14, 2018, https://www.rogerebert.com/reviews/unbroken-path-to-redemption-2018.
10. "9/11 Day Ambassadors—Tina Hansen and Michael Benfante Interview," YouTube, https://www.youtube.com/watch?v=f-_dSQPBcF0.
11. Alex Bryant, "What Do the NFPA 1582 Physical Fitness Requirements Say?" FireRescue1, August 5, 2020, https://www.firerescue1.com/health-wellness/articles/what-do-the-nfpa-1582-physical-fitness-requirements-say-O7AnVpUgU22nrYIA/.
12. New York City Council, Minutes of the Proceedings for the Meeting of Thursday, October 17, 2019, https://www1.nyc.gov/assets/dcas/downloads/pdf/cityrecord/stated_meeting_2019_10_17.pdf.
13. Dean Balsimini, "Number of Fatalities from NYC Fires Jumped 16 Percent in 2021, Data Shows," *New York Post*, January 8, 2022, https://nypost.com/2022/01/08/number-of-fire-fatalities-in-nyc-jumped-16-percent-in-2021/.
14. Marcus Costello, "Female Firefighters Fired Up About New Gender Quota," The Feed, March 22, 2017, https://www.sbs.com.au/news/the-feed/article/female-firefighters-fired-up-about-new-gender-quota/twpsl9g8v.
15. Roger Gonzalez, "FC Dallas Under-15 Boys Squad Beat the U.S. Women's National Team in a Scrimmage," CBS Sports, April 14, 2017, https://www.cbssports.com/soccer/news/a-dallas-fc-under-15-boys-squad-beat-the-u-s-womens-national-team-in-a-scrimmage/.
16. "Back in the Saddle," *Forbes*, December 3, 2001, https://www.forbes.com/asap/2001/1203/064_print.html.
17. Dan McLeod, "Lance Armstrong Finally Admits to Doping, Lying in Interview with Oprah Winfrey," *New York Post*, January 18, 2013, https://nypost.com/2013/01/18/lance-armstrong-finally-admits-to-doping-lying-in-interview-with-oprah-winfrey/.

Chapter 9: The Married Man

1. Jon LaPook, "Following a Couple from Diagnosis to the Final Stages of Alzheimer's," CBS News, August 12, 2018, https://www.cbsnews.com/news/60-minutes-alzheimers-disease-following-a-couple-from-diagnosis-to-the-final-stages/.
2. Michael Reagan, *Lessons My Father Taught Me: The Strength, Integrity, and Faith of Ronald Reagan*, Kindle edition (West Palm Beach: Humanix, 2016).

3. Ibid.
4. Ibid.
5. "Full Text: Ronald Reagan's Christmas Love Letter to Nancy, Read at Former First Lady's Funeral," KTLA 5, March 11, 2016, https://ktla.com/news/local-news/full-text-ronald-reagan-christmas-love-letter-to-nancy-read-at-former-first-ladys-funeral/.
6. "Transcript: Nancy Reagan on 'Larry King Live,'" CNN, February 5, 2001, https://www.cnn.com/2001/ALLPOLITICS/stories/02/05/reagan.lkl.trans/.
7. Ben Chapman, *The 5 Love Languages for Men: Tools for Making a Good Relationship Great*, Kindle edition (Chicago: Northfield Publishing, 2015).
8. Ibid, 15.
9. Ibid, 127.
10. Ibid, 12.
11. Jeff Foxworthy, "The Rules of Marriage," YouTube, https://www.youtube.com/watch?v=w_g3uqin8Ck.
12. "Jeff Foxworthy on Marriage, Parenthood, Being a Grandparent and Finishing the Race," Family Goals with David Pollack and Pastor J, November 29, 2021, https://www.buzzsprout.com/1838367/9544660.

Chapter 10: Man as Provider

1. Ellen Hendriksen, "Failure to Launch Syndrome," *Scientific American*, May 18, 2019, https://www.scientificamerican.com/article/failure-to-launch-syndrome/.
2. William Bradford, *Of Plymouth Plantation: 1620–1647*, The Plymouth Colony Archive Project, http://www.histarch.illinois.edu/plymouth/bradford.html.
3. Shelby Steele, *The Content of Our Character* (New York: Harper Perennial, 1991), 170.
4. Laura Wronski, "Axios/Momentive Poll: Capitalism and Socialism," June 15, 2021, https://www.surveymonkey.com/curiosity/axios-capitalism-update/.
5. "Chris Gardner: The Homeless Man Who Became a Multi-millionaire Investor," INews Guyana, December 5, 2016, https://www.inewsguyana.com/chris-gardner-the-homeless-man-who-became-a-multi-millionaire-investor/.
6. Ibid.
7. Chris Gardner, "The Speech Every Student Must Hear," YouTube, https://www.youtube.com/watch?v=CtTK-_-IsJc.

8. Josh Hawley, "What the Porn Industry Is Selling Men Is a Lie," *Tucker Carlson Tonight*, December 20, 2022, https://www.foxnews .com/video/6317572046112.
9. Melanie Arter, "Schumer: 'We Have a Population That Is Not Reproducing on Its Own with the Same Level That It Used To,'" CNS News, November 16, 2022, https://www.cnsnews.com /article/washington/melanie-arter/schumer-we-have-population -not-reproducing-its-own-same-level-it.
10. Gabriel Hays, "Schumer Dragged After Pushing Citizenship for Illegal Immigrants as US Birth Rate Drops," Fox News, November 16, 2022, https://www.foxnews.com/media/schumer-dragged -after-pushing-citizenship-illegal-immigrants-us-birth-rate-drops.
11. Janine Puhak, "Instagram Influencer Defends Her Large Family, Calls Out Racism," Fox News, February 12, 2020, https://www .foxnews.com/lifestyle/instagram-influencer-large-family-defends.

Chapter 11: The Knowledgeable Man

1. Finlay Greig, "100 of Homer Simpson's Most Hilariously Hair-Brained Quotes," INews, October 9, 2020, https://inews.co.uk /light-relief/jokes/homer-simpson-quotes-152562.
2. "Booker T. Washington Delivers the 1895 Atlanta Compromise Speech," History Matters, September 18, 1895, https:// historymatters.gmu.edu/d/39/.
3. Sheila Marikar, "Why T.I. Decided to Save His Old Atlanta Neighborhood (and How He's Doing It)," *Inc.*, August 2008, https:// www.inc.com/magazine/201808/sheila-marikar/how-i-did-it -rapper-t-i-clifford-joseph-harris-jr-buy-back-the-block.html.
4. Kimberly Fain, "The Devastation of Black Wall Street," JSTOR Daily, July 5, 2017, https://daily.jstor.org/the-devastation-of -black-wall-street/.
5. "W. E. B. Du Bois Critiques Booker T. Washington," History Matters, https://historymatters.gmu.edu/d/40.
6. Booker T. Washington, *The Negro Problem*, Project Gutenberg EBook, February 14, 2005, https://www.gutenberg.org/files/15041 /15041-h/15041-h.htm.
7. "Du Bois Critiques."
8. Ta-Nehisi Coates, "The Tragedy and Betrayal of Booker T. Washington," *The Atlantic*, March 31, 2009, https://www.theatlantic .com/entertainment/archive/2009/03/the-tragedy-and-betrayal-of -booker-t-washington/7092/.

9. TRA Committee Hearing Transcript, February 6, 2015, https://cga
.ct.gov/2015/tradata/chr/2015TRA00206-R001030-CHR.htm.

10. Ben Carson, *Hannity*, Fox News, February 15, 2013.

11. Benjamin S. Carson, Achievement.org, https://achievement.org
/achiever/benjamin-s-carson/.

12. 2013: Ben Carson's Speech at the National Prayer Breakfast,
February 7, 2013, Blackpast, https://www.blackpast.org/african
-american-history/2013-ben-carsons-speech-national-prayer
-breakfast/.

13. Dr. Ben Carson Presidential Announcement Full Speech, C-SPAN,
May 4, 2015, https://www.youtube.com/watch?v=ulsA8aFOkRs.

14. Lori Higgins, "Detroit Renames School Honoring Ben Carson,
Removing Honor for Trump Appointee," Bridge Michigan,
November 17, 2022, https://www.bridgemi.com/talent-education
/detroit-renames-school-honoring-ben-carson-removing-honor
-trump-appointee.

15. Andrew Hughes, "We Worked for Dr. Ben Carson. We Know Dr.
Ben Carson. Canceling Him Is Just Not Right," Fox News, February 8, 2022, https://www.foxnews.com/opinion/worked-ben-carson
-know-canceling-just-not-right/.

16. Jason L. Riley, *Maverick: Thomas Sowell, a Biography* (New York:
Hachette Book Group, 2021), 3–4.

17. Ibid., 5.

18. Ibid., 67.

19. Ibid., 252.

About the Author

Lawrence Jones is a host on the Fox News Channel. Prior to joining Fox News, he was the editor-in-chief of *Campus Reform*, hosted his own radio show on TheBlaze Radio Network, and served as a contributing host for TheBlaze TV.